THE WHY & HOW OF
WOODWORKING

THE WHY & HOW OF WOODWORKING

MICHAEL PEKOVICH

The Taunton Press

The Taunton Press
Inspiration for hands-on living®

63 South Main Street
Newtown, CT 06470-2344
Email: tp@taunton.com

Editor: Peter Chapman
Copy Editor: Seth Reichgott
Art Director: Rosalind Loeb
Jacket/Cover Design: Rita Sowins
Interior Design: Michael Pekovich
Design Template: Rita Sowins
Layout: Michael Pekovich
Illustrator: John Hartman
Indexer: Cathy Goddard
Photographers: Michael Pekovich and Rachel Barclay except as follows:
  p. 34 (bottom left) courtesy of Seth Janofsky; pp. 66 (except top left), 67, 69 (bottom left, bottom right)
  Andy Engel, courtesy of *Fine Woodworking*; pp. 91-95, 205, 208, 209 Dillon Ryan, courtesy of *Fine
  Woodworking*; p. 197 Mark Schofield, courtesy of *Fine Woodworking*; pp. 210, 211 Steve Scott, courtesy
  of *Fine Woodworking*

The following names/manufacturers appearing in *The Why & How of Woodworking* are trademarks:
Bluetooth®, DMT®, iPhone℠, Lie-Nielsen®, Minwax®, Pigma Micron®, Pottery Barn®, SealCoat®,
Starrett®, Veritas®, Waterlox®, Zenith®, Zinsser®

Library of Congress Cataloging-in-Publication Data

Names: Pekovich, Michael, author.
Title: The why and how of woodworking : a simple approach to making
  meaningful work / Michael Pekovich.
Description: Newtown, CT : The Taunton Press, Inc., [2018] | Includes index.
Identifiers: LCCN 2018015441 | ISBN 9781631869273
Subjects: LCSH: Woodwork.
Classification: LCC TT180 .P39 2018 | DDC 684/.08--dc23
LC record available at https://lccn.loc.gov/2018015441

Printed in the United States of America
10 9

ACKNOWLEDGMENTS

There are too many people to thank for their support, not just in the last two years of writing this book, but also along the 30-year journey that led to it. To my wife Rachel, daughter Anna, and son Eli, thank you for your patience and encouragement. You are my rock and I could not have done this without you.

I have had so many mentors along the way, and it's a shame that so few of them know the impact they have had. I've learned from every one of the hundreds of articles that I have had a hand in bringing to life at *Fine Woodworking* magazine, and the authors I've had the good fortune to work with. I am grateful for the wit and wisdom of Gary Rogowski, the patient uncompromising drive of Christian Becksvoort, and the creative genius of Garrett Hack. The great engineering minds of the craft, Steve Latta, Will Neptune, and Michael Fortune, have shaped my approach to problem solving in too many ways to count. Chuck Miller, a former editor of *Fine Homebuilding* magazine and all-around creative genius, has forever been my role model in being positive, creative, and open to the joys that life can bring, though I'm still working at it.

John Tetreault, you continue to inspire me to try and view the craft through the creative lens with which you approach it. Jon Binzen, you possess the greatest mind and pen to ever document the craft, and of all the voices I carry with me in my head as I work, yours is the clearest and the one I'm most apt to be listening to.

To every student I've had the good fortune to work with, I thank you for your questions and trust and for your patience along the rather steep learning curve I'm still climbing as a teacher. To Bob Van Dyke and Marc Adams, thank you for taking a leap of faith and letting me loose in front of students at your schools.

To Peter and Rosalind, thanks for your patience, trust, and flexibility in allowing me to make a book in the only way I knew how to make it. To John Hartman, a good friend and long-time collaborator at *Fine Woodworking*, thank you for putting so much effort into the amazing illustrations that bring this book to life. I confess that I enlisted you because I knew that you couldn't help investing far more than you reasonably should have into this project.

I also want to thank one of the true unsung heroes at The Taunton Press. For 20 years, I have relied on the immense artistic and photo-editing talents of Bill Godfrey to make so-so photos look good and good photos look brilliant. He is the reason why the photography in *Fine Woodworking* is head and shoulders above any other magazine. Thank you, Bill, for making this book more beautiful than it deserved to be.

CONTENTS

INTRODUCTION

This endeavor began with two questions: Does the world actually need another woodworking book, and what exactly do I have to contribute to the conversation? I decided that the answer to the first question had a lot to do with my ability to answer the second question. I've been going about this craft for 30 years or so, and I'm as passionate about it now as I have ever been. More to the point, I'm having more fun and am happier with the results of my efforts now than ever before. While it's taken me a while to get here, I don't think it necessarily has to take that long for you. And that's why I'm here.

Working alone in my shop for that many years has instilled in me the empathy and understanding of the everyday struggles that woodworkers face. We are an intrepid lot. Years of crafting articles at *Fine Woodworking* magazine have provided an unending Master's education in designing and building furniture. That experience has been informative and inspiring, but humbling as well as I became aware of the many great woodworkers who are carrying the craft forward. For a long time, I felt that I didn't really have anything to add, but as I struggled to find my way, I realized that all of us have something we can share.

My efforts in teaching have prompted me to rethink how I go about building in order to pass along the best methods and strategies that I can. Not only does that make me a better teacher (I hope), but it also has shaped the way I go about work in my shop. Any advice I offer, I do so because it not only works for me but also for the students endeavoring to master the craft as well.

Finally, taking the time to document my work on a daily basis for the past few years has opened my eyes to the beauty and grace of the building process that is so much a part of what we make but is most often hidden from view. It has prompted a more personal approach to photography, with the aim of communicating the passion that is inherent in the pursuit of this craft.

All together, these experiences combine to make this book what it is, as well as making me the woodworker I am today. They continue to drive my joy in working with wood and in helping to blaze a path for others who are making the journey as well.

Whenever I'm asked, "Oh, what kind of furniture do you make?" I'm always at a loss for words. There is just too much wrapped up in the experience to be able to distill it down to a single sentence at a typical social function for the benefit of a half-interested audience. This book is my answer to that question. It's my hope, and my suspicion, that it just may be the answer to that question for other woodworkers as well. This book is for you, and whether you are standing at the trailhead or have already knocked a few peaks off your list, we are all on the same path, and I welcome your company.

CHAPTER 1

MAKE SHOP TIME MATTER

Work on getting the most from your time in the shop, and you'll work toward building the work you want to make. If there's one common theme in this book, as well as in my approach to the craft, it's that everything is connected. Bring a mindfulness into the shop, attack even the smallest task with the same focus and resolve, and not only will it add up to good work, but it will also invest your time in the shop with the meaning that you're there for. From sharpening to sweeping up to emptying the dust collector to buffing off the last coat of wax, do it well and you'll find a flow where work gets done in an efficient way. Along the way, you'll have more fun, too. Fun may not be the right word, because I think it's more than that. You'll be closer to realizing your aim in heading out to the shop in the first place, because how you go about the work you do and your satisfaction with the final result go hand in hand. Focus on the little stuff, because in the end, it's all little stuff.

What follows are the "rules" I depend on to get the most out of my time in the shop. While I'm not always entirely successful in following all of them, at the least they offer a way to get back on track if things do start to get away from me. I hope they can help you make the most of your shop time as well.

1. IT'S NOT THE NUMBER OF HOURS, BUT HOW YOU USE THEM

I have to balance my shop time with my duties as an art director, teacher, and writer, but I don't think of woodworking as a hobby. It's much more than that for me and for every woodworker I've met. However, for the vast majority of us pursuing the craft, shop time is limited. We carve out precious minutes between our family and job and household duties, maybe feeling a little guilty for stealing away to the shop whenever we can. Or you might be trying to explain to people, including yourself, why in spite of a fresh college degree, you're working odd jobs in order to get into your shop on occasion and make things out of wood.

Since I became serious about the craft in college, my aspiration has been to become a full-time woodworker. I haven't hit that mark yet, and I'm not sure it's still a goal. Even the full-time professionals I know spend a good portion of their shop time on jobs that pay the bills, and the opportunity to do the work they really want to be doing is just as elusive for them as it is for the rest of us. So the real answer doesn't lie in getting more hours under our belts, but in how we make use of the time we do have.

2. MAKE IT A HABIT

When most of us say we've been working on a project for six months, what we probably mean is that we spent five and a half months of that time not working on it.

When most of us say we've been working on a project for six months, what we probably mean is that we spent five and a half months of that time not working on it. When I'm asked how can I get so much woodworking done with such a busy schedule, the most important reason is that I make a point to go into my shop just about every day. That rarely means a full day and often means as little as 15 minutes or so. The important thing is to get in there. No matter how slowly a project may feel like it's progressing, it will be moving forward if you continue to chip away at it.

One of the real killers of momentum is an extended break. The rhythm, the train of thought gets lost. You return to a stack of parts that don't look entirely familiar and an idea of how to proceed that's a little foggy. This is when I make the most mistakes: "I know there was a reason I was holding off on this, but it seems like a good thing to tackle right now." And once I jump into it, the memory clears and I remember why that wasn't such a good idea. And once I'm fixing mistakes instead of moving ahead, it definitely feels like I'm moving backward.

3. DO YOUR THINKING AWAY FROM THE SHOP

Thinking of your next move can eat up a lot of precious shop time, so I try to do as much of that as I can before I get into the shop. I've solved more joinery problems and brainstormed more jigs while lying awake in bed than at any other time. It's a great feeling to work out a solution to a construction challenge and then head to the shop, put it to the test, and have it work out. While our focus might be on getting into the shop, the hands-on work actually represents a smaller portion of building a project than you might think. The choreography is what counts: linking the individual tasks into a logical workflow, and being able to see the long view in accomplishing what you need to and the order in which to attack it.

The need to break down the job into bite-sized tasks to fit our shop time might feel like a burden and concession to a busy life, but it actually helps to build an important

BREAK IT DOWN

If the first step is to get out to the shop, the next step is to begin to make good use of that time. It's really important to complete a task at every outing. The worst thing is to have to stop midway and then try to figure out where to pick up the next time around. The key is to break down larger jobs into manageable tasks. If I'm dovetailing a bunch of drawers, I may only get around to scribing all of the shoulders. Maybe the next time around I can start in on the tails.

Make a list if you need to. Try and get down as many separate steps as possible. That way, if you have just a short amount of time, you can knock one off, and a longer session may mean a few check marks. What if you don't have anything specific to work on? Get out there anyway. Sweep the floor or change a bandsaw blade or sharpen a plane. Any of those tasks will make your next trip to the shop that much more productive.

As much as we want to get into the shop, it's just as important to sit down and really think about what we want to make and whether it's the best choice when we stop to consider every other potential project on the list.

skill. Even with all the shop time in the world, you still have to have a plan. If you're in the shop a lot, that plan sometimes gets written on the fly, or you may even begin to outpace it and find yourself painted into a corner that you need to work your way back out of. So take advantage of the time off and use it to invest in making the best use of the shop time you do get.

Start to think not just one or two tasks out but plot the entire course. As an example, every issue of *Fine Woodworking* magazine contains a couple of project articles. There's not enough space to cover the entire building sequence in six or eight pages, so what I try to do is create a series of stepping stones to get you from one task to the next. While I try to provide the dimensions you need in order to build the project, the really valuable information is the order of operation. What you are getting is an insight into how a master craftsman approaches building, the logic behind all of the seemingly disconnected steps. "Why are they cutting joinery before shaping curves? Why are they waiting until the case is built to start on the doors and drawers? Why are they finishing parts before they are assembled?" That's where the gold is. Pay attention to

that and you'll become a better woodworker without practicing another dovetail. Even the most complex project can be broken down into a series of simple steps; learning to make that road map for yourself will make it a lot easier and more enjoyable getting where you want to go. All of that can happen during drive time or in that next meeting you're stuck in.

4. MAKE SURE IT'S WORTH BUILDING

When we rush into a project, sometimes we shortchange the design process. I've been there. I've pulled a design together on the fly just to have something to make. As I got deeper into the project, I'd find myself wondering if what I was making was worth the effort I was putting into it, and I would start to lose steam. As much as we want to get into the shop, it's just as important to sit down and really think about what we want to make and whether it's the best choice when we stop to consider every other potential project on the list. When in doubt, I turn to the purpose of what I'm making. What need does it fulfill and how important is it? The urge to get out and make is often about our desire to find that bliss in our connection to the craft. To consider the purpose of what we're making connects us to the people who will be using it. With that focus in mind, I tend to be a little more thoughtful and patient with the design process. And I'm usually happier with the results and, just as important, feel better about the time that I've invested in the project.

5. WHY THE LITTLE THINGS ARE THE "BIG THING"

I admit I've spent a lot of time in the shop rushing through or putting off "unimportant tasks" to get to what I really wanted to be doing. I'd do a rush job on sharpening or try to get the most out of a tool before touching it up again. I'd sharpen just one chisel or plane iron instead of all of those that needed it. Scuffling through piles of sawdust and shavings on the floor, I'd begrudgingly pull out the push broom and carve a clean swath down the center of the walkways. I'd eke out one more milling session with a dust collector that I knew to be almost full, and work around the clutter on my workbench, clearing off just a large enough spot to fit the task at hand. I'd hit a wall then hit the lights, leaving a shop in total disarray, only to be greeted by it the next time I snuck back in with just a few minutes to get something done. And so goes the cycle. If you've been here, or are here, you know what I mean. Shop time is precious, and we want to make the most of it.

Today, I still fight the fight, but my working conditions are generally improved, and, more important, my mindset is more focused and able to do good work as well. So what changed? Well, for me, the biggest factor was the decision to treat every task in the shop as equally important.

For a very long time, I'd adhered to the practice of giving my shop a good clean at the beginning of a big project. Of course, I'd tackle a lot of small projects in between, which meant I was working in a mess most of the time. I realized I had equated the completion of a project with the satisfaction I was looking to achieve in the shop. I viewed any task not directly related to building as a waste of time, an enemy standing in the way of finding my bliss. What I came to realize was that if I wanted more of my time in the shop to be meaningful, then it was up to me to invest the meaning into that time. While my aim has always been to work with clear focus and intent, I decided to broaden the types of tasks that were "worthy" of that focus.

I know it sounds a little simplistic to say "just decide that everything is meaningful, and suddenly every task will be enjoyable." While I may not like to sharpen, I like using sharp tools. Emptying the dust collector is a pain, but firing it up at the start of a big milling job knowing it can handle the whole task is pretty satisfying. Walking into a shop with a swept floor, clear work surfaces, and tools tucked neatly away and at the ready makes for a good day of work. When my shop is clean, I tend to want to keep it that way. I don't think anyone would disagree with those things, but it doesn't necessarily mean we do what it takes to get there. But here's the thing: Each of the "unimportant" tasks has a direct impact on the "important" work you're there to do. A sharp tool, a tuned machine, and an ordered shop all combine to create an environment and a mindset where you can do good work and enjoy doing it.

Take a minute to think about that spider web of interconnectivity, and it's not a great leap to see that if all of the tasks in the shop are interdependent, then each of those tasks—from cutting a dovetail to emptying the trash—is an equally important part of

Each of the "unimportant" tasks has a direct impact on the "important" work you're there to do. A sharp tool, a tuned machine, and an ordered shop all combine to create an environment and a mindset where you can do good work and enjoy doing it.

WASH YOUR HANDS, PUT ON AN APRON, OR TURN ON THE MUSIC

When you get to the shop, make a break from your daily routine, your stress, all the voices swirling in your head. Bring your full attention but leave everything else behind, even if you're in there for just a few minutes. For me, it helps to have a ritual of sorts. I fumble with the Bluetooth® speaker to get the music going, and then I put on my shop apron and make sure all the tools are in the right pockets. If I don't have time to do those things, then I probably don't have time to be in the shop.

Those little actions help to get me in the zone and help to do away with the occasional nagging thought that I should be doing something else. With the music playing and my apron on, I'm in the shop, body and mind. Even washing your hands before you get to work can act as a break from your day and help to focus your thoughts on the way into the shop.

So the real question is not hand or power, but where exactly does the trailhead begin for you? There's no one right answer, nor is the starting line fixed.

the overall process. And each is equally worthy, and demanding, of our full attention. So, yes, taking care of the little stuff will help to make shop time more enjoyable and productive, but there's an added benefit. It's getting to the mindset that "it's all shop time." Every minute in the shop is a hard-earned minute for most of us. So whether I'm sweeping or putting tools away or fitting a door, it's all good.

6. SHAVINGS OR SAWDUST?

Hand versus power. In a way, it's a non-argument, but I feel obliged to address it considering that it has to do with why a lot of us pick up the craft in the first place. Throughout the history of woodworking, if there were any type of grunt work involved that you could get away from doing yourself, you'd avoid it. That meant using cheap labor like the guys stuck in the sawpit turning logs into lumber. Later it was waterpower, steam, electricity, and so on.

Up until recently it was understood that if you could afford a machine to make your life easier, you'd buy it. Until then, you'd make do with what you had. It was a basic equation of time versus money. A mortising chisel is cheap, but a mortiser is fast. I cut my teeth following the path of great studio makers like James Krenov, Tage Frid, George Nakashima, and Sam Maloof. All of these masters depended on machines to

get them as far as they could go and only then turned to hand tools to take them the rest of the way.

Today, there's a movement toward hand tool–only work, where the focus is not so much on speed or efficiency but on the experience of making. It's about the connection between mind and hand and tool and wood without a tablesaw blade spinning away in the middle of everything. It's the difference between rushing down a highway to get where you're going versus taking a walk through the woods, where it's not about the miles you cover but the steps you take.

I love to hike, but I also like to drive to the trailhead. During one trip to the Sierras, there had been a late heavy snow and the road to the trailhead was blocked. We had to hike a couple of miles on asphalt with heavy packs, and by the time we hit the trail I had more than a few blisters going. In *A Cabinetmaker's Notebook*, Krenov wrote that while he could handle the lumber prep with hand tools, by the time he was done he'd be too worn out to do the fine work required to complete the project. I prefer to tackle tenons at the tablesaw, while Matt Kenney, a good friend of mine, often cuts them by hand. When I asked him why, he said that it gets him to the workbench that much faster.

So the real question is not hand or power, but where exactly does the trailhead begin for you? There's no one right answer, nor is the starting line fixed. Some, like myself, may start with power and adopt more and more hand methods as our skills in-

While my hand tools represent the heart of my shop, my machines are a close second. I have as much of a personal relationship with my bandsaw and tablesaw as with my handplanes. The skill and concentration required to saw a fair curve at the bandsaw is equal to that required by just about any other tool in the shop, powered or unpowered.

crease. Others may be drawn to the romance of shavings wafting through the sunlight only to decide that they need to get a move on if they're going to have a chance to cross any projects off of their list.

Starting out, I had just enough hand tools—a backsaw, chisels, block plane, and layout tools—to cut a dovetail and chamfer a corner. It was a good ten years before I picked up a handplane, and I did a lot of work during that time that I'm still proud of. Since then, however, hand tools have come to play an increasingly important role in my work. My surfaces are flat and smooth, the edges crisp, and the joinery as tight as I can make it. But more than that, hand tools also help to instill a rhythm to my work and an enjoyment in the process.

I've always hated sanding, and still do, but to spend a morning getting sharp and an afternoon making shavings is a day well spent. So for me the question of hand versus power doesn't really come up other than in choosing the right tool for the task at hand. Use your gut as a guide. If four-squaring a board by hand feels like a slog and you have a different way to go about it, fire away and don't feel guilty about powering up a planer. On the other hand, if there is nothing about using a router that is remotely enjoyable to you, find another way to cut a molding that you will enjoy—and don't feel bad that it will take you longer to do it.

No matter which tools you choose to arm yourself with, the big picture doesn't really change: building with function and beauty in mind, having a process that gets you from start to finish with the least amount of angst and frustration, and finding the zone where your best work gets done and you have the most fun doing it. Pretty simple.

7. OUR MINDSET MAKES A DIFFERENCE

I was recently listening to Andrew Hunter, maybe my favorite woodworker, lecture on the wonders of Japanese handplanes, and I was struck by a concept he mentioned. He talked about how the spirit of the plane maker was invested in the plane and by using the plane the maker's spirit along with Andrew's was invested in the work. I know that the term "spirit" as applied to tools and woodworking might be tough to get a handle on, but there is something really important contained in that thought. If we substitute "energy" for "spirit," then it starts to make a lot of sense.

Everything we do to transform a tree into a piece of furniture involves expending energy. From jointing and planing and milling to cutting joinery and finishing, each step requires an investment of energy. Our state of mind can have a big effect on the nature and quality of that energy. If we rush, if we are frustrated or stressed or preoccupied with events outside of the shop, then all of that is transferred into the piece we are making. If we are fighting a dull tool or stepping around a cluttered shop, it all shows up in the finished project. In the literal sense, it's impossible for us to do our best work under those circumstances. In addition, they compromise our ability to make the hundreds of intuitive decisions that need to be made while we build—from how we tackle a problem to deciding when a blade needs to be sharpened. It's certainly difficult, if not impossible, to enjoy the work we are doing. The focus and intent with which we go about business in the shop has a tangible effect on both our work and the product of our efforts.

Trust that all the little stuff, the extra efforts we can choose to make throughout a project add up and will pay off in subtle but important ways in the end. The concept holds true whether we are using a tablesaw or a handplane. So it's not really about the tools we choose to use, but the mindset with which we put them to use.

If we rush, if we are frustrated or stressed or preoccupied with events outside of the shop, then all of that is transferred into the piece we are making. If we are fighting a dull tool or stepping around a cluttered shop, it all shows up in the finished project.

FIRST THINGS FIRST

Tools are our connection to the wood. Their condition dictates the conversation we have and our ability to communicate our intentions. Something as mundane as sharpening has such a big impact on our experience and the precision of the work we can do, that we can't help but begin there even if all we really want to do is head to the shop and make some shavings.

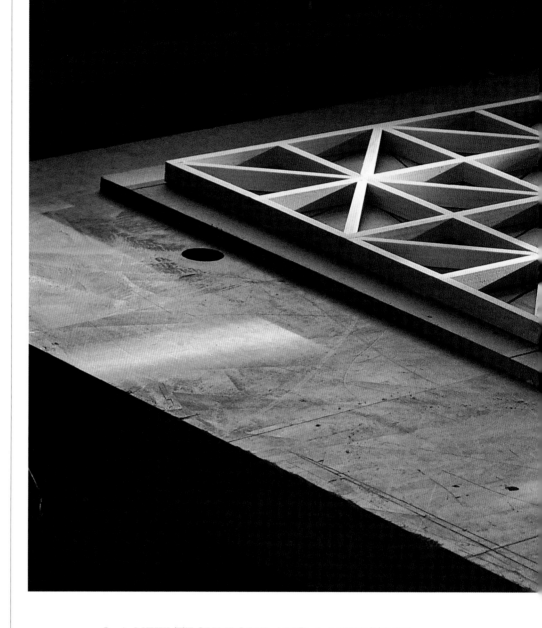

By limiting the number of new challenges in a piece, we give our-selves a chance to hone our skills on the techniques we've already tackled and still leave enough mental bandwidth to allow us to give full attention to the unique challenge at hand.

8. A NEW TECHNIQUE AND A NEW TOOL WITH EVERY PROJECT

In craft, in art, in life, the notion of moving forward is ingrained in our consciousness. We want to improve our skills and our knowledge, to go beyond where we have been in the past. In woodworking, we tend to measure progress one project at a time. If we repeat a project we've already made, there's a sense of standing still, but if we take too far of a leap on a new project, we can be left in free fall. Hence my rule of one new technique and one new tool per project.

My first dovetailed box was a momentous achievement. I was left with a feeling of accomplishment but also with the notion of never wanting to cut another dovetail. Today, a dovetail is just a dovetail, and while dovetails show up frequently in my work, my attention is usually on new challenges. By limiting the number of new challenges in a piece, we give ourselves a chance to hone our skills on the techniques we've already tackled and still leave enough mental bandwidth to allow us to give full atten-tion to the unique challenge at hand. The new challenge might be a particular joint or

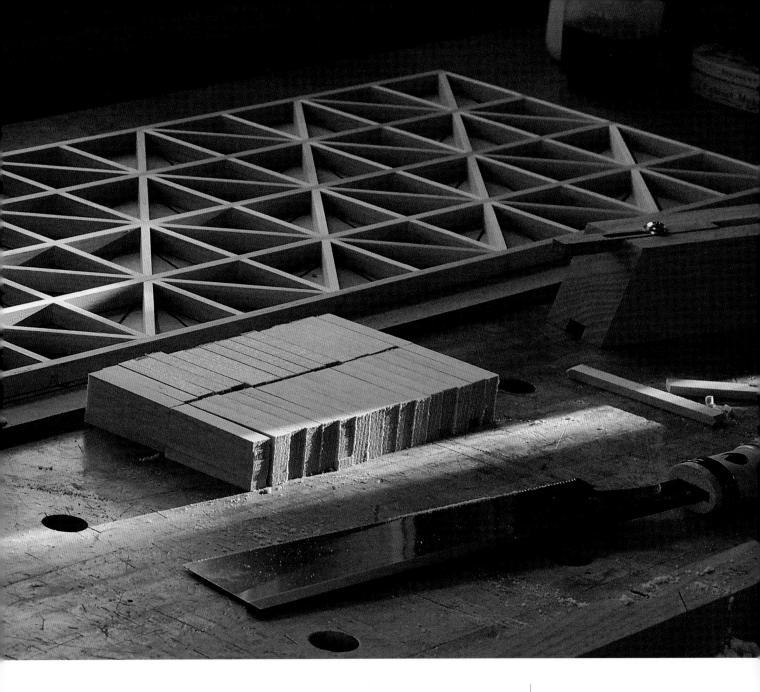

a decorative detail. It might be working with an unfamiliar wood or trying out a new finish. Any one of those would definitely draw my interest, but addressing all of them at once could leave me chasing my tail.

Another benefit of sticking with a single new element at a time is that it gives you a chance to get to know the technique or wood or finish process, so that you can add it to your mental catalog of skills or problem-solving solutions. Almost all of my current work involves techniques and details that I've used in past work. And as my skills grow, so does the arsenal of solutions that I can throw at any given project.

Building a set of tools can follow the same path. I'm often asked what tools are needed to get started. The answer is always, "Well, where do you want to get started?" Once we get going, the basic set comes together pretty fast (see chapter 3 for my "big 12"). After that, rather than thumb through a tool catalog for ideas, just let the project at hand dictate what comes next. In this way, a new technique often goes in tandem with a new tool. The next thing you know, your tool chest will be bursting at the seams and you can add another project to your list.

9. RETHINK PERFECT

The perfect dovetail, the perfect finish . . . or grain match or carving, or whatever. We can beat ourselves up pretty well and set some high standards for the work we're attempting. I like the notion of perfect, but I have spent some time rethinking and reprioritizing exactly what I'm shooting for. Too often we're choosing an unrealistic ideal. At times we all fall prey to the desire to make "real" furniture, whatever that might mean. Unfortunately, if that goal is to mimic the accuracy of a CNC machine with a kit of hand tools, we're going to fall short.

Worrying about the finish line, where we'll end up, doesn't really help us to get there. So instead, keep your head down and focus on each small task at hand. Complete each one to the best of your ability and move on to the next. My most successful pieces are the ones where everything seemed to flow smoothly from task to task. Instead of thinking in terms of "perfect," I like to think of a successful piece as "fully realized." An awkward term, perhaps, but what I mean is that I make an effort to make sure that a piece is what it needs to be—and no more. Sometimes trying to do too much is just as bad as not doing enough.

10. DON'T RUSH, BUT DON'T STAND STILL

If you've ever listened to a child learning to play the piano, you've probably been struck by an overall lack of rhythm, starting, stalling, repeating, rushing, only to stall again. When I was leaning to play the guitar, my instructor advised me to play at the tempo of the most difficult section of the song I was learning. So rather than rushing through the parts I knew well only to slow down at the more difficult parts, I played the entire song at the slowest tempo necessary to maintain an even rhythm. As the difficult parts became easier, the entire tempo gradually sped up. The important thing is that there was a consistent momentum, a rhythm that connected the individual notes.

The same concept applies to woodworking. Find the tempo where you feel as though you're moving at a constant pace from task to task, a tempo that allows you to invest the necessary focus for each task without feeling as if you are rushing through some tasks and hitting a wall with others. When you find it, you'll probably also find that your work has a consistency that was missing before. And while it may seem that you are working at too slow of a pace, as your skills progress, your speed will too. The important thing is that you will always feel in control of the process and of the quality of work that you are doing.

Slowing down also gives you time to think between tasks. It's often said that half the time in the shop is spent thinking of what to do next. I definitely know that feeling, but I try to minimize that as much as possible. When putting a clamp away or clearing off the bench, instead of rushing through it (or putting it off entirely), use the time to think about the next task at hand. Instead of standing and staring for five minutes, the same thinking gets done within the flow of the work that is being done. You don't get something done faster by rushing. It's only by finding the patience to maintain a deliberate pace that work progresses at its fastest. Don't rush and you won't need to stand still. Both are counterproductive. Find your groove and you'll be surprised at how easy the process is and the level of quality that you are capable of working to.

The first time through a project there's a lot of stopping and thinking, a lot of second-guessing and fretting about details. If you make it again, the path will be clearer. It will be easier to think multiple steps ahead so that there is a coherent movement forward

You don't get something done faster by rushing. It's only by finding the patience to maintain a deliberate pace that work progresses at its fastest.

DON'T RUSH, BUT DON'T STAND STILL

during construction. It may even feel that you're not trying as hard, and you might worry that it won't turn out as well. Instead, there will probably be a subtle sense of life to it that was missing from the original. That stopping and starting during the first try yields to a more relaxed flow, and that flow invests itself into the finished product. You don't necessarily need to attempt everything you make twice in order to experience that. After a while, as skills become ingrained, you'll begin to see a clearer path to the finish line on each new piece you attempt, and you can begin to invest that same sense of rhythm in every project. It begins in the details, all those small tasks that seem so endless, then progresses to finding that path where they all begin to connect, until you can build a road map through a project that will get you where you want to go at a steady pace without any detours along the way.

11. RESPECT THE MITER

Miters are simple, but miters are really tough to get right. Unlike a dovetail, which is fairly simple to cut but strikes fear in our hearts, the humble miter can catch us off guard if we're not careful. The miter's seeming simplicity can lull us into not doing our best, giving us a sense that somehow it's undeserving of our full effort. And once we slide down that slope, we're in for some hurt.

There are lots of aspects of woodworking that seem just as simple, just as undeserving of our full attention. The problem is that it's all simple stuff when you get right down to it, so if you take the path of selectively assigning import to this or that task, the whole will begin to suffer, but it will be difficult to pinpoint exactly where the problem lies. Take the time, invest the effort in every task, and it will become a habit. You'll have less decisions to make along the way and the end product will benefit as well.

12. SOMETIMES YOU JUST NEED TO LET IT GO

Something happens when we lose momentum on a project: Other ideas and new projects start to come to mind. When that happens, the current stalled project can become a stumbling block to getting onto other things that are starting to grab our interest. Still we try to tough it out, especially if we've invested materials and a good amount of time to get this far. And sometimes that's all it takes.

I find that if I can spend a good chunk of time, maybe a few hours on consecutive days, I can start to find the groove again, and once I can see some progress, the finish line doesn't look so far away. Other times, though, I've learned that sometimes it's best to let it go and start in on something fresh. Now, I never really think in terms of giving up; I usually think of it as more of "maybe I'll just put this aside for the time being…." Every woodworker I know has at least one of those projects hanging around the shop, but just because they haven't seen the light of day (and maybe never will), it doesn't mean that they were a failure or without benefit. Every project we attempt, every joint we cut, every tool we sharpen informs the next effort at the same task. After I had revamped my shop and I was still trying to figure out where everything should go, I finally decided to build something and let the course of events dictate where I wanted the tools that I needed and how to begin to organize things based on the tasks at hand. That project fell victim to one too many missteps, but it ended up serving a valuable purpose on its way to the kindling pile. And so it might just be time to set aside that stalled project in the corner and jump to something new.

Every project we attempt, every joint we cut, every tool we sharpen informs the next effort at the same task.

THE MARK OF THE MAKER

At first, we tend to think of any evidence of the building process that we see as defects—mill marks, tearout, sanding scratches, gaps in joinery, sapwood that was unnoticed before the first coat of finish went on—and our focus is on removing them. That's not a bad thing, but beyond that, there is a point where the marks left by a skilled hand can be a bonus.

A crisp chamfer from a block plane, the scallops on a drawer bottom from a scrub plane, the precise scribe line left by a sharp marking gauge: They all affect the final product in an important way. They are the marks of the maker that mostly go unnoticed but add up to instill a certain vitality and life to the work we do.

CHAPTER 2

DESIGN

If we weren't concerned with an end product, the answer to what constitutes meaningful shop time would be easier. It would be finding that bliss in the connection between the maker and the material: or more simply, just taking shavings. While that may be a big part of it, and perhaps the primary siren call that got you started in the craft of woodworking, if you decide to stick with it, the product of your efforts will take on more meaning.

And that's where design begins to play an important part in your work. Not design as in making something crazy or original but in making something that does its job well and looks good doing it. Time in the shop is about our connection to the craft. The finished object is about our connection to others. What we make matters, because if we do it well, it will affect the world in a positive way. It might be in a small, quiet way, but it's an important one just the same. And so design —the determination of the final product, its beauty, its usefulness—really can't be separated from the making. Like it or not, we're all tasked with being designers. The good news is that we're all capable of answering the challenge.

1. BUT I CAN'T DRAW

Woodworkers tend to be engineering-minded folks, so the notion of designing furniture can be intimidating. Common complaints are, "I'm not creative," "I can't draw," "I'm not an artist." So why not think of it as engineering a piece of furniture instead? Better, right? I know that making a piece of furniture usually requires a big expense and a big investment of time, which means it's tempting to start with a proven design that will guarantee a good chance of success. That's actually not a bad place to start. I built a number of projects based on the work of makers I was inspired by.

While using existing designs as a springboard for original work is a great idea, simply limiting yourself to what's already been built out of fear of messing things up defeats the purpose and possibilities of making something by hand. 99% of furniture design involves sizing a piece to its function and building it soundly. But the other 1% is the fun stuff. It's about building for the user, thinking about the little things that can make a big difference.

You know a good piece when you see it, so the trick is to give yourself a chance to see what you're making before you make it. That's really what it's all about. A full-size drawing or mock-up will give you the chance to say too big, too small, too clunky or skinny, or whatever. It's tough to have the courage to say that about a project you've spent six months building, but with a mock-up you can be ruthless. There are some rules of thumb that can get you past some common road bumps, but rules and formulas are only there to get you close. Your eye is the ultimate judge, and the more you give yourself a chance to use it, the better your work will be.

2. THERE ARE NO MAGIC FORMULAS

The notion of a magic number or formula or ancient ratio that will guarantee beautiful work is very appealing. A number that unites the planets with the pyramids with the bones in your hand sounds like a cool thing. The golden mean, the golden rectangle, the Fibonacci series, phi—there is something to be said for all of these, as well as for many other proportioning systems, but here's the thing: They are all there to help you get to something that looks pleasing or resolved. They are all intended to get to something that looks good to your eye. Formulas won't necessarily guarantee success, and the proportions they recommend may not be best suited to the function of the piece you're building. So I recommend learning to trust your eye.

The problem with following any formula is that it can make you less confident and less likely to listen to your own intuition: "The proportion is correct, so it must be good . . . I guess . . . ." That's not to say there's no truth to the beauty of mathematics, but you don't necessarily need math to do good work. There are good sources of information on the subject, so I won't cover them in this book, partly because I don't use them often, but more to the point, I think that there are more important considerations that will more directly lead you to the work you'd like to be doing.

For instance, a very useful tool is what I call the socks and underwear construct. Simply put, let the purpose dictate the scale and proportions of a piece. A dresser should be sized for the clothes it needs to contain. A tea box may be beautiful, but if it's too small to hold tea bags, then it's not a great tea box. Ok, I'll admit it. This is not a random example. I made a tea box for one of my daughter's

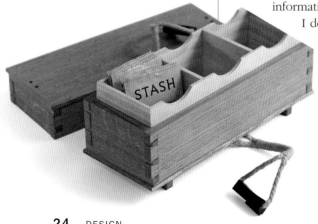

I recommend learning to trust your eye. The problem with following any formula is that it can make you less confident and less likely to listen to your own intuition.

BUILD WITH A PURPOSE

A friend asked me to make something for her. "What?" I asked. "Anything you want to make." I told that her I needed more, I needed a starting point. I needed a reason to make something. Do you need a cabinet? Should it sit on the floor or hang from the wall? What room will it live in and what is it going to hold? Answer those questions and I'm well on my way to the scale and proportions of the piece, as well as the combination and size of doors, drawers, or shelves and such.

A bathroom cabinet, a bedroom nightstand, an entry hall table. The location starts to affect the flavor, the wood, the style, the level of use. Is it a public piece or a private piece (a really important distinction). Is it a piece for use by others, for family, for visitors, or for yourself alone? More and more of the design puzzle pieces fall into place by determining the function, the relationship to the user. In doing so we are determining what the piece will be rather than merely considering how it should look.

Instead of viewing function as a constraint, I find that I need it as a springboard for inspiration. Even on spec pieces that aren't aimed at a particular end user, I still try to define its use and let that guide the design. Focus on the inside, the core of the piece, and the outside will resolve itself. Design is not about surface decoration—it's about creating. And what we are creating are functional objects.

elementary school teachers, and, well, the interior was just a hair small to fit the foil-wrapped tea bags it was intended for. As a solution, I ended up trimming each bag slightly with a pair of scissors, so that they all sat perfectly snug in the box. I never did find out what happened when she went to replenish the box with new tea bags and found that none of them fit, but I still cringe at the thought of that too-small box today. So fit the function first.

The other primary consideration is the scale of the human body, the ergonomics of a piece. We interact with furniture and functional objects every day, and if the scale is off, it's not a pleasant interaction: a chair too high or too low, a table where you smash your knees on the aprons, a tea box too large to comfortably carry with one hand.

None of this is particularly earth-shattering, but if you think about it, solving the problem of function and ergonomics goes a long way toward making a piece that performs its intended function well. Start there and you're already most of the way home. While we may think of "design" in terms of deciding how something should look, it's really more about determining what something should be.

3. JOINERY AS INSPIRATION, NOT LIMITATION

I first studied furniture making in art school. Many of the students stepping into a woodshop for the first time were incredibly creative but lacked any knowledge of wood and how to work it. The designs they'd come up with initially were often unbuildable without a lot of compromises to the design. In their frustration, it was understandable that they considered joinery as an enemy of realizing their designs. While I didn't have quite the same resentment of the medium, I did find that as I became a better craftsman, I became a better designer as well. Rather than view joinery as an afterthought, it became an important part of my design palette.

Philosophies vary when it comes to thinking about how to balance building and design. Michael Fortune, a brilliant designer and craftsman, approaches the task of design first: He determines how his project will look and then figures out a way to construct it without compromising the design. Michael is also an incredible engineer when it comes to constructing his unique visions.

The biggest influences on my work are pieces where the joinery is exposed and becomes part of the decorative aspect of the work. It's a way to build in the look of a piece rather than tack it on later with veneer or inlay or molding and such. For that reason, I tend to think in terms of joinery when working up a design. Before starting in on a piece, I almost always (OK, always) have a really good idea of how everything is going to go together. Each small detail of construction will have an impact on the overall look and functionality of a piece, so a lot of my design time is spent running through a catalog of joinery options that I can throw at any given design challenge. As each solution comes forward, it begins to dictate the following solution, so that by the end of the design process, the remaining details tend to fall into place by themselves. During the designing and building of a project, we make hundreds of small decisions along the way. By linking those decisions together, they can work toward a more resolved design.

However, I do find that focusing too much on the joinery solutions I'm familiar with can leave me in a bit of a rut. So it's always fun to throw in a new challenge now and then that might take a little time to figure out. That way, not only am I building on past efforts, but I'm paving the way forward with each new project as well.

As I became a better craftsman, I became a better designer as well. Rather than view joinery as an afterthought, it became an important part of my design palette.

4. DRAW, DRAW—AND DRAW SOME MORE

I have a number of sketchbooks cluttering my house, each one with an ink pen threaded through its spine. In them, I make quick, small sketches, with just a few lines to conjure the idea of a piece. A while ago, I was in bed with the flu and unable to head out to the shop. So I occupied my time by filling up a sketchbook with drawings, each maybe an inch square—too small to try and sweat the details, but enough to capture an idea. A rectangle became a cabinet or a bookcase. A vertical line became a divider, horizontal lines became shelves. The combination became doors or drawers, so that in quick, shorthand form, a dozen iterations of a piece could be conjured in just a few minutes. Fast, fast, fast. And fun.

When I revisited the sketchbook, my first thought was that I'd just designed more furniture than I could build in a lifetime—a somewhat depressing thought. But as I looked further, it became apparent that not all of the designs were worth building. A few here and there, however, caught my eye. Maybe it was just an errant squiggle of a line that suggested something more by accident than anything else, so I drew a few more sketches to try and capture that spark of an idea. And once I got hold of it, it was just a matter of fanning it into a flame and carrying that energy through the rest of the building process. So drawing has now become a habit, and instead of deciding what to build next, it's now more a matter of looking for ideas that demand to be built. I still have more ideas than I can put to use, but going into a project with a design that I'm excited about is a wonderful thing.

Studying furniture making in college, I had gotten to the point where I'd make a project per semester. At the start of one semester though, my instructor suggested that instead of making one piece, why didn't I spend the semester just designing pieces. I was a little hesitant because my joy was in building and the school shop was the only access to a woodshop that I had. Still, I decided to give it a go. However, after the first design was complete, I dropped everything and began to build it, and there went the semester. Wisdom is wasted on the young. It's taken a few years, but I'm finally putting that idea into practice.

TO CAPTURE A SPARK, START SMALL

A small sketch has a lot going for it. It's fast, so you can knock out a bunch in one sitting. You can fit a lot of them on a single page, which saves paper and has the added benefit of allowing you to look at a lot of ideas at once. Small doesn't let you get lost in the details. You have room for only the basic structure of a piece, which is a great place to start.

You may not think you can draw, but you can draw well enough to design. Here's how to start:

Get a small blank sketch book with a good paper: 6×9 is big enough, but you can go bigger if you'd like. My favorite pen is a Pigma Micron® 05 archival ink felt-tip pen.

Start by filling a page with stacks of short horizontal lines, maybe an inch or so long. This is important because you can draw the lines with just a flick of the wrist. Straight and parallel. Now try some vertical lines of the same length. Quick but accurate, and loosen up on that grip a bit—this is sketching,

not engraving. Now try diagonal lines in each direction; don't be afraid to rotate your sketchbook to make it easier.

Now you're ready to draw some furniture. Start with a tall rectangle and then subdivide it in as many ways as you can think of. It could be a bookcase or a tall cabinet. It could have drawers, doors, shelves, or a combination of any or all of them.

Draw until you fill up a page or run out of gas. Put it aside, and when you pick it up again, start on a fresh page. Once you have a few pages filled up, take a quick look back and see if anything catches your eye. If something grabs you or sparks an idea, try redrawing it a few times. Play with the proportions, the spacing of the elements, and see if the idea picks up a head of steam. Then let it sit a while longer. Before you know it, you'll have a book full of ideas in various stages of evolution. Keep going until one of those ideas demands to be built, and you're ready to go.

5. FANNING THE SPARK INTO A FLAME

So how exactly do you get from that blip on a page to a finished piece of furniture? The good news is that finding the spark was the toughest part; trust it and it will get you the rest of the way home. While the idea may seem vague, it's actually a more concrete idea than you might suspect. The first step is to focus on the function: What will it do, what will it hold, how will we interact with it? That will begin to determine the scale, proportions, and features of the piece. From there you need to get a sense of how the piece will live in the real world. When I'm working out a project, I'll look at everything around me—a filing cabinet, a water cooler, a cardboard box (anything I can look at and say, no, that's too tall or too wide or too short or too narrow). By comparing the idea in your head with real-world objects, you can start to dial in exactly what you want. When I arrive at the ideal size of a piece, it's rare that I know the exact dimensions of it until I measure it after the fact. The key is that it fit what I had in mind. With that in hand, you can begin to draw to scale.

Start with a small rectangle scaled to the finished dimensions of the piece. As an example, for a bookcase 30 in. wide by 42 in. high, start with a rectangle measuring 2½ in. by 3½ in. Now redraw your rough sketch to scale and you're on your way to transforming that spark of an idea into something real. You'll quickly know if your idea translates to the actual proportions of the piece, and you may need to adjust your design to fit or rethink the proportions of the project.

The next step is to go full size. This might be a drawing on plywood or cardboard, or you could break out the glue gun and drywall screws and go at it. For shallower work like a wall cabinet, I'll often make a full-size drawing of just the front view. A drywall square and a handful of permanent markers are all you need. If something doesn't look right, turn the drawing over and try again. For a case piece, I'll typically mock up the front and one side—you need to see it from only one angle. Stand it up and add a piece of plywood for the top and you'll have a good view of it. From there it's just getting rid of the things you don't like about it. Now that you have a better view of the piece, you'll know when something's not right. The task now is to trust your eye and fix everything that's wrong with a design until you're left with only good stuff.

When I'm working out a project, I'll look at everything around me—a filing cabinet, a water cooler, a cardboard box (anything I can look at and say, no, that's too tall or too wide or too short or too narrow).

To see how a squiggle of an idea holds up to real-world dimensions, make a page-size drawing. A 1:6 or 1:8 scale drawing can accommodate a typical piece of furniture on a single page. I usually start with a front view to dial in the basic proportions and then go to a ¾ view to get a better idea of the overall size of a piece. After that, I'll start in on a full-size mock-up.

SEE IT BEFORE YOU BUILD IT

Design demands the courage to look at your work with a critical eye. One way to lower the stress is to work with mock-ups—something made quickly from foamcore, plywood, MDF, or rolls of butcher paper. Hot-melt glue and drywall screws hold everything together, and a permanent marker makes drawer and door layout a breeze. Quick and easy is the key: You are less likely to hesitate when assessing your progress.

Too big, too small, too narrow, too wide? Trust your first response. Don't stare at the mock-up until it looks right, just go with your first impression. Trust it. Make the changes and look again. Then forget about it. Put it in your house, let it catch you by surprise when you come into the room, and listen to those quick first thoughts before they disappear in a puff of smoke. What is not right, what is not right, what is not right . . . ? Get rid of all of those hiccups and you'll be left with something that is as it should be.

ALL YOU COULD ASK FOR IN A WOOD

Some love affairs can last a lifetime. You would be forgiven if you started in with cherry and never left it for another wood. Cherry is close to the perfect wood. Its color is a rarity: not too dark, not too light, but a beautiful red that deepens with age. It is a crime to stain cherry. The only challenge is in convincing a client to wait six months for that salmon-colored piece of furniture you just delivered to transform into something close to what they had imagined. Cherry is a wonderful wood to work, but beware—the slightest figure can quickly lead to tearout. Yet the figure in cherry is worth the work. Not the tight curl of tiger maple, figured cherry is more akin to the flowing auburn locks of a 1940s movie star—all satin and shine. It's a wood you can dress up in high period style or use to highlight a simple Shaker piece. Like maple, it will burn if your tablesaw blade isn't sharp, and it will chip out if your jointer and planer knives are dull. A hurried surfacing routine will lead to a blotched finish, but a well-prepped surface will shimmer under a coat of oil.

Each species is more than a color or texture. Each wood has its own character, its own point of view. Each wood demands a different touch, a different tool, a different mindset that affects not just the making, but what you make of it as well.

6. FALL IN LOVE WITH WOOD

Fall in love. Fall in love with a wood, with a tool. Fall in love with a style or with the work of a maker you admire. Let that passion drive what you make, and how you make it. But definitely fall in love with wood.

Each species is more than a color or texture. Each wood has its own character, its own point of view. Each wood demands a different touch, a different tool, a different mindset that affects not just the making, but what you make of it as well. To say that a piece of furniture is available in three different woods is misleading. To make it in a different wood will change its essential character so that it is, in essence, a different piece altogether. Whereas white oak demands crisp, bold chamfers, flame birch inspires a softer, pillowed approach. Work with a wood enough and you begin to know it, begin to think in it. It will begin to inform what you make and how you make it.

Pine is a softwood. That sounds easy, right? But not if you've worked with it. Pine is insistent on a sharp edge; anything less will tear and rip the grain, any heavy handling will dent the surfaces. Pine is demanding, but its rewards are many—the golden shimmer left by a sharp handplane, the smell that fills the shop, the patina that comes with age. It is a wood that is wonderful left unfinished, or with a light coat of blonde shellac at the very most. It will inspire you to learn to sharpen, to invest in Japanese chisels and saws. It will inspire quiet designs. Its lightness and warmth invite touch. It weathers the dents and dings of use well. It is not a wood that hesitates to be used and will quickly become part of the daily life of a home, not something closeted away in fear of scratches or reserved for company. Pine is a warm, worn comfort.

A WOOD WITH A SPLIT PERSONALITY

White oak is the permanence and strength of a stone foundation. It is wise and patient. Quartersawn oak carries with it a split personality in the rigid order of its tight, straight grain married to the wild, romantic undulations of its ray fleck. It is at once restrained and untamed. Don't compare working with oak to working with other woods, or you may never venture to give it a try. Resign yourself to it instead and you will build a relationship that is well worth the effort. I will go for months working with nothing else until its hardness becomes the norm. When I do come up for air with a new project, say, in cherry or walnut, it is a wonderful thing, but if I stray too long I begin to hesitate about going back to oak.

You cannot be tentative with oak. Its end grain will not give in to half-hearted paring. So when you are fitting joints, you have to be bold; you must jump in and get the job done, or you'll be left with faceted humps of waste that will keep joints from ever seating. Your handplanes must be deadly sharp, and your card scraper ever ready. If you pound away with chisels, you will be rewarded with folded or fractured edges. However, if you stay on the path of paring wafer-thin slices, you will be rewarded with glass-smooth end grain and razor-sharp edges.

Oak is not refined, but it is not without its grace. No other wood provides the mass to a project that oak can. Chamfers take a hard crisp shine, but the open grain of oak doesn't encourage delicate profiles. Oak is elemental. It invites curves, but they must be sound and true. Oak is about structure, not ornamentation. Oak will decorate broad flat surfaces with ray fleck where other woods will lose form. Try to substitute for oak in an Arts and Crafts piece and it will fall flat. Then again, to attempt a highboy in oak is to call down doom upon you.

IN COMBINATION

Combining woods is much more than an exercise in color theory. The more you understand the nature of different woods, the more effectively you can combine them. As a starting point, try to factor in the grain of a wood along with its color. Flame birch and tiger maple differ in color, but their distinctive figures complement each other well. Oak and sycamore can be very similar in color, but the lace-like grain of quartersawn sycamore adds a sparkle to the pairing. The inky black lines of spalted maple tie in the light-colored wood with darker woods like wenge for an exciting effect. Without the lines, the contrast between the woods is too extreme for my taste.

Walnut lives and dies by its unique chocolate color. It's one of those woods that is either trending and painfully overpriced compared to the last time you bought it, or it's in the doghouse and lumberyards can't give it away. Walnut is a muse to many great makers, like Sam Maloof and especially George Nakashima, whose live-edge legacy not only lives on but is thriving again today. Walnut is a joy to work, maybe my favorite wood to work. It carves well and polishes to a wonderful luster. It complements other woods nicely; I've used it with oak and cherry, though maple proves too far a stretch unless the walnut is used sparingly as an accent wood. As a primary wood, you have to be committed to the color and accept that it will dominate the piece. So for me, it's only an occasional indulgence.

7. THERE'S NO SUCH THING AS BAD WOOD

A very small percentage of wood species is sold commercially. If you keep your eyes open to alternative sources of lumber, you can be rewarded with some amazing wood. A cabinet by Seth Janofsky, a northern California woodworker, is one of my favorite pieces (left). It is made from knotty pine, which is not normally associated with fine furniture. Seth was able to put its graphic quality to great effect, and it reads like a strikingly contemporary piece of furniture. Since seeing Seth's work, I tend to keep my eye out for knotty pine boards at my local home center, and they've ended up in a number of cabinet backs.

In the same way that there's no bad wood, there's no guarantee that a spectacular board will result in a great piece. Highly figured wood can have a tremendous impact, but harnessing that power takes a strong will and a disciplined approach. On a chimney cupboard, I used an incredible figured cherry board for door panels and drawer fronts but built the rest from straight, quiet riftsawn cherry. The tight, straight grain of the riftsawn boards framed the wilder stock and prevented it from overwhelming the cupboard.

A basic rule of thumb is that the larger the areas of color, the subtler the contrast should be. Highly contrasting woods make excellent accent points on a piece, but too much of a good thing is definitely not a good thing. On a wall cabinet, oak drawer fronts add subtle contrast to the ash case, while pine kumiko and ebony pulls add a little more pop.

8. FALL IN LOVE WITH A STYLE

I've fallen in love with a few myself. When you do, really dig in. Find those pieces you want to build and get going. And then dig a little deeper. If you like Stickley furniture, search out the real thing and not just catalog reproductions. Auction websites are a great source (I used to hunt down auction catalogs at flea markets in pre-Internet days). Then head to a museum and try to take a look at original work. The scale will probably surprise you. Examine the hardware, the details, the finish. Let those begin to inform the work you do. Get down to the essence of what you like about the style, and you'll begin to build and design from within the style. And then look into the roots of the style.

For the origins of the Arts and Crafts style, I hang out in the medieval section of the Metropolitan Museum in New York, drooling over pierced carvings and intricate iron hardware. Try to find what the makers you admire were influenced by, where their ideas came from. There are layers of influence in every piece made today. A good maker is a historian and an interpreter. Garrett Hack, a Vermont furniture maker and farmer, distills the essence of the Federal style and brings it into a contemporary conversation, so that people who may not think they like the style will find the spark of appreciation in his work.

Lose yourself in a style, and it may have you in its grip for your entire career. Every style is such a deep well that hitting bottom is never a concern. I came into Arts and Crafts through the work of Greene & Greene, architects who designed houses and the furniture that went in them. Their Pasadena homes, the Gamble House in particular, are monuments to the style. Later, I discovered the work of Gustav Stickley, which has become synonymous with the Craftsman style for most Americans. But if you stop there, you're missing the really fun stuff. The movement was a loosely defined style that included many makers from many countries. Taken as a whole, it will provide you with a rich palette to work from.

When I relocated to New England, I fell for the beautiful simplicity of the furniture made by the Shakers. Devoid of adornment but filled with the spark of creativity, its austerity points to 20th-century furniture styles. Delving into the style, I became familiar with cherry, maple, and butternut, and with the notion that local woods can offer all the variety one would need (assuming one lived amidst an unending hardwood forest). I learned to use hand tools efficiently and relearned the basics of furniture construction as well. Both of those lessons drive the work I make today.

The work of James Krenov and George Nakashima opened my eyes to the wonderful design possibilities that the mid-century modern style has to offer. It was the last great design movement featuring solid-wood furniture and combined brilliant designers with talented makers. After 70 years, much of the work is still too "modern" for many tastes, but the echoes of the style will resonate for many years and generations of makers to come.

9. CRAFT A PHILOSOPHY AND LET IT DRIVE YOUR DESIGN

It's probably not a coincidence that the styles I like most are those that are driven by an underlying philosophy. The Arts and Crafts movement was a rejection of Victorian excess and the dehumanization of the Industrial Revolution. It championed a democratic approach to life, and the notion that a home should be built using local materials, that a piece of furniture should be designed for a specific place in a specific room. The idea that furniture was transportable from house to house was unheard of and led to the

Get down to the essence of what you like about the style, and you'll begin to build and design from within the style.

FINDING YOUR VOICE

I would say that my path toward a more personal style began with the decision not to work in any style at all, but that's a little misleading. While it's true I don't consciously build in a particular style, my work is greatly influenced by all of the styles that I've worked in. For the most part, I don't build in the Shaker or Craftsman styles, but it's easy to connect the dots through those styles to get to where I'm at today. The white oak and exposed joinery typical in Arts and Crafts furniture and the playful asymmetry of Shaker design found their way into a recent wall cabinet. There's a residue of influence that infuses my work even when I'm not aware of it. Those truths that inspired me and drove my work then have turned out to be evident now, even when I've left the specifics of those styles behind.

classic built-ins found in Craftsman bungalows. This notion was taken to its highest form in the work of Greene & Greene, where pieces of their furniture today are still described by the house for which they were built.

The Shaker movement was also a rejection of worldly influence. Unnecessary adornment was discouraged and utility was of prime importance. Other than chairs and brooms and seed boxes, furniture was not built for sale. It was built for use by individuals within a community. There are examples of sewing tables that are identical in every way except for their height because they were made for two different people. While reproduction catalogs have distilled the style down to a small number of stereotypes, a visit to a Shaker village will open your eyes to an unending variety of work. My favorite objects are odd, idiosyncratic pieces not constrained by fashion or proper proportions, but delightful and brimming with the essence of the maker nonetheless.

The mid-century style railed against traditional notions of design and stagnant norms of fashion and how we should live. There was a breaking away from the past and an optimism for the future that created startlingly original architecture and furniture.

While we're drawn first to how the furniture in a style looks (its structure and details), it's important to get down to the philosophy behind why it looks the way it does. In doing so, not only can you begin to build more authentically in that style, but also to craft your own philosophy. With that in hand, design becomes more than just deciding how something should look, flitting from one idea to another. Your work will have a momentum from piece to piece, a voice that slowly develops. There will be a resonance to your work that speaks to the maker and person you are.

In every case, the design of these movements was not about surface ornamentation or driven by fashion whims of the moment. It was driven by a life view and connected to a larger cultural or communal movement that imbued the work with a deeper resonance that transcends fashion or time so that its vitality is still evident and relevant to us today. If you are looking to instill a meaning, a permanence, a truth in your work, looking to these movements may provide a path forward.

The problem with jumping around is that it's difficult to stay anywhere long enough to really nail what you're after.

10. REPETITION: IT WORKS FOR DESIGN AS WELL AS DOVETAILS

In the past, I would typically jump from style to style, always wanting to try something new. There's nothing wrong with that approach, and sometimes you just need to get some pieces out of your system, whether it's a Morris chair, a Massachusetts lowboy, or a Federal card table. The problem with jumping around is that it's difficult to stay anywhere long enough to really nail what you're after. For a while now I've tended to stay in the same territory. While it sometimes feels a little too close to standing still, I've slowly and quietly gotten better at what I'm doing. I use a lot of elements that have shown up in previous works, with just a single new element or two introduced with any given piece. With just about any accomplished artist or musician, there's a long steady arc to their evolution. While I am not aiming for greatness in my work, the notion of moving forward is really important and I find the only way I can do that is step by small step.

BREAK THE RULES

On more than one occasion, I've found myself asking, "But can I do that?" It's usually in response to wanting to try something even though it doesn't seem to be the "correct" thing to do. I'm a big fan of adhering to basic rules of design, but sometimes you have to put them aside and say, "No, hand-forged strap hinges and a kumiko panel have no place in a mid-century modern writing desk." And then do it anyway.

Yes, rules are great. They can be really important guides in making work that you like to live with, but the rules are there for you. Sometimes the spark of intuition is a better guide. It's easy to get stuck in the notion of building furniture that looks "real." You know what I mean: When someone comes over to your house and says, "Wow, that looks like you could buy it in a store!" After the first gasp of indignation, part of you thinks, "Cool, it is a real piece of furniture." The problem is that anything we make with the intention of it looking real is usually compromised by the notion. Yes, develop your eye, but trust your gut as well.

We're in the shop working hard, either not getting paid to do it or not getting paid enough. We're starting with raw materials and through our efforts and intentions we bring something into the world that had yet to exist. The very best we can hope for is to capture a little of our spirit in the piece along the way. Any spark of life that a finished piece can have has to come from you. So go ahead and worry about scale and proportion and function and sound construction, but keep an ear out for those wacky ideas that won't go away, and when no one is looking, give in to them and see what comes of it.

11. ART VERSUS CRAFT

Our work should be beautiful, but it's important to be aware of the distinction between art and craft. Making art is an act of self-expression. There are no limits, no rules, and no demand placed on the final product. Craft by its nature is something else. Craft is about function. Craft needs to work for a living. A chair might be beautiful, but if it breaks when you sit on it or is uncomfortable, then it is a bad chair. That is the essence of art versus craft.

First and foremost, we should be building with function in mind. While beauty is important to the user's experience, it isn't the sole concern. Because of that, craft may never ascend to the lofty realm of "art," but it can play just as important a role in our lives and in the lives of the people who utilize our work.

While we are resigned to simply look at a painting on a wall, we interact with crafted objects. Furniture, boxes, coffee mugs, quilts, and mittens—we live with these objects, and they inform our lives in a sometimes small, but intimate way. So build with a purpose, with a use in mind, with a user in mind. In doing so, you can experience an increasingly rare opportunity to truly connect to other people. This is not a small thing, nor a small responsibility. For many of us that are somewhat communication-challenged, the opportunity to give such a gift to a friend or provide for a customer offers a way to connect to others in a way that words often can't.

12. SOMETIMES YOU JUST HAVE TO GO FOR IT

While I'm a big proponent of sketches and mock-ups to dial in a design on important projects, sometimes, when no one is looking, I head to the shop with just an idea. It might be a cabinet, a chest, or a small table. I'll grab some stock, hold it up, give a quick thought (too long? too thick? too wide?), and proceed from there—not allowing myself to stare too long, but just chasing down the spark of an idea through the twists and turns of the building process. Along the way, I'll listen to those fleeting thoughts and trust them. It's a safe place to take all of those chances that can get you into trouble in a bigger project.

When you give your intuition a chance to make a call, it's usually the right one, and giving yourself an opportunity to follow through on those hunches will lead to a more confident approach to building in the future. At the end, I'll have absolutely no idea of any of the exact dimensions. Admittedly, the results of these endeavors may still be a little off the mark when they're done, but I tend to really like them. They have an energy that can get stamped out in a more thought-out design process. There's a spark and spontaneity that is impossible to capture in a project designed for a paying client. These imperfect pieces, these rough sketches or studies, often drive later, more refined, and carefully planned work.

So design becomes not just a multi-step process from sketch to mock-up to plan to construction, but a process that flows through multiple projects in order to find its resolution. Every project I make is an accumulation of thoughts and details and lessons learned from previous projects. I find that the more chances I take, the faster my work moves forward. Quick "unimportant" projects allow me to take more of those chances without worrying too much about things going wrong.

When no one is looking, I head to the shop with just an idea. It might be a cabinet, a chest, or a small table. I'll grab some stock, hold it up, give a quick thought (too long? too thick? too wide?), and proceed from there.

DESIGN IS AS MUCH ABOUT GETTING IT WRONG AS GETTING IT RIGHT

Yes, I worry about building something that isn't perfect. The problem is that I don't think I've actually built a piece that was. That's not to say that I'm not happy with any of them: If they do their job well and add a little personality to the mix, then they earn their keep as far as I'm concerned. That said, I can look at just about anything I've made and think about what I would change, or "fix," the next time around. The consolation is that I wouldn't be able to conceive of those fixes if I hadn't made those pieces in the first place. And those frustrations can be put to use to help improve future projects.

Every piece I make today is informed by the near misses of the past, because each one has taught me a valuable lesson, whether it's a design detail, or a reminder of how wood movement is more than just theory, or the importance of lumber selection or surface prep. Maybe it was a design that I had rushed through in order to get in the shop. As much as I may aspire to build something wonderful, the next piece is going to be the next piece. If I want to get further, I have to accept that and determine to make it as best as I can, examine it with a clear eye, and let it guide me toward that better piece beyond it.

CHAPTER 3

HAND SKILLS

I'm often asked what the prerequisites are for the project classes I teach. Regardless of the complexity of the task at hand, the requirements are always the same: Get comfortable with a basic set of hand tools and the rest is easy. To have success, and a sense of control while building, you need to be able to scribe and knife accurate layout lines, get a chisel sharp and use it with precision, and have the confidence to use a backsaw without stressing out. For surfacing and shaping, you need to bond with your block plane, because it's the tool you'll use most frequently. Learn to hone and use a card scraper as well. This simple tool will save you from hours of sanding. Finally, eventually, get a smoothing plane sharp and tuned for fine shavings. While this is often the first tool we think of when getting into hand tools, it has the steepest learning curve, and you can get by without it for a while. That said, once you do master it, its benefits are many, so don't take it off your list altogether. Getting started is simple. Gather a basic set of tools, learn how to get them sharp, and get to work.

12 ESSENTIAL HAND TOOLS

THE BIG 12

- *Marking gauge*
- *Combination square*
- *Marking knife*
- *Bevel gauge*
- *Backsaw*
- *Coping saw*
- *Chisel set*
- *Shoulder plane*
- *Block plane*
- *Card scraper*
- *Spokeshave*
- *Smoothing plane*

Twelve tools. It doesn't sound like a lot, and I'm not implying that you won't benefit from owning more, but start here, get to know them, and get them to work for you, and you will have come a long way toward doing the work you want to do.

I started out mostly using power tools, but I've learned that even if you have every conceivable machine, you still need hand tools to produce your best work. I still use machines for the heavy lifting of milling and dimensioning lumber. There are also a number of joints that machines can handle quickly and accurately, leaving me with the energy to tackle the rest of the project. I save my hand tools for where they really make a difference: layout, cutting dovetails and through tenons, as well as fitting joints and surface preparation. These tools (OK, and a few more) are what I depend on to take my work to a higher level. You probably already have some of them, and the rest you can pick up over time. And it's well worth the effort, because using them will help you to make better furniture.

There is another aspect of handwork that has a big effect on the work we do. It's a notion that easily gets lost in the romance of plane shavings or in the historic pursuit of traditional tools and techniques. Working with hand tools offers a more intimate and immediate connection to the material we work with, and that connection can determine not just how we make something but what we make as well.

In addition to these tools, you'll also need a sturdy workbench. You may be harboring visions of a massive tank of a workbench complete with expensive hardware, but if you don't have a bench yet, think about saving the dream bench for later. Start with something simple—a bench you can build in a weekend without spending a lot of money. Bolt on a cast-iron vise, and you're ready to go. Get some work under your belt, and then decide on what your ideal bench should be. A sturdy bench is a start, but it shouldn't be a stumbling block that keeps you from getting to the work you want to be doing.

TOOLS FOR LAYOUT

MARKING GAUGE

COMBINATION SQUARE

A cut line is better than a pencil line because it provides a precise location and line for starting a chisel or handsaw.

Accurate layout is an essential part of making fine furniture, and it's just as important for power-tool work as it is for handwork. That's because regardless of the tools you're using, you need precisely located and square joints. If you're just starting out in woodworking, these should be the first hand tools you buy.

MARKING GAUGES excel at cutting a line parallel to the edge of a board, which is vital for laying out accurate tenons, mortises, and the baseline for dovetails. A cut line is better than a pencil line because it provides a precise location and line for starting a chisel or handsaw. Gauges with a knife or cutting wheel cut cleaner lines than do pin gauges. Good wheel gauges are easier to find, so I'd start there; I recommend one like the Tite-Mark or Veritas® wheel gauges for your first.

A COMBINATION SQUARE is indispensable for penciling or knifing a line at 45° and 90°. It's important to get a good one, like those made by Starrett®, because it will be accurate out of the box and will stay that way. The 12-in. model is a workhorse, long enough to mark wide boards or across multiple pieces at once. It's a good square to get first, but I've found a second, 6-in. version is just as handy. Because of its small size, it fits better in your hand and is easier to use when laying out joints in tight places and across end grain.

MARKING KNIFE

BEVEL GAUGE

PAINTER'S TAPE

You also need a sharp **MARKING KNIFE**. I've owned and used many different types, but the one I reach for time and again is a chip-carving knife. I like the blade's double bevel, which lets me mark on either side of the blade. And the bevels extend the entire height of the blade (the cross-section is triangular), so I can rest the blade against the side of the workpiece and strike a line exactly adjacent to it. The blade also is long, thin, and stiff, so it fits in tight places without flexing.

Because it has a pivoting blade that can be locked into any angle, a **BEVEL GAUGE** is useful for transferring angles from plans to workpieces and for setting tablesaw blade angles. However, you'll probably use it first to lay out dovetails, a task it is perfect for. When buying a bevel gauge, look for two things: First, the blade should lock down tightly, so it doesn't move accidentally. Second, the nut used to lock it down shouldn't get in the way of using the gauge (a frequent problem with the wing nut used on some gauges).

Finally, while it may not seem important enough to add to the list, **PAINTER'S TAPE** is a must-have for me. Even the most accurate layout doesn't do a lot of good if you can't see it. I lay painter's tape down before dovetailing or mortising and peel away the waste to show me exactly where to cut. And where not to cut.

TOOLS FOR JOINERY

JAPANESE AND WESTERN BACKSAWS

For me, the long-term benefit of the Western saw is the handle shape. The pistol grip naturally aligns the sawblade with your forearm, which makes it easier to cut consistently.

Dovetails are the hallmark of craftsmanship, and the effort to cut them by hand is well worth it because of the speed and versatility it offers. However, even if you use power tools to cut all of your joinery, hand tools are still the best way to fine-tune the fit. For hand-cut dovetails and tight-fitting tenons, I recommend a backsaw, a coping saw, a set of chisels, and a shoulder plane.

With its top-mounted stiffener, a **BACKSAW** is designed to do one thing: cut straight lines for tenons and dovetails. The two types of backsaws are the Western saw, which cuts on the push stroke, and the Japanese saw, which cuts on the pull stroke. Because even an inexpensive Japanese saw comes razor sharp right out of the box, and beginners usually find it easier to start a cut on the pull stroke, I recommend it to those choosing a first backsaw.

Even if you switch to a Western saw later, you'll still find a lot of uses for the Japanese saw, like cutting small parts and flush-trimming pegs. For me, the long-term benefit of the Western saw is the handle shape. The pistol grip naturally aligns the sawblade with your forearm, which makes it easier to cut consistently. The more consistent your cuts, the more confident you'll be with your saw, and that's the real key to success.

The basic **BENCH CHISEL** is probably closest to the heart of good work. There are so many tasks you can accomplish and ways to use a chisel that it becomes an extension of your hand and your closest connection to the wood as you work. Start with at least four: ¼ in., ⅜ in., ½ in., and ¾ in. After you have the basic set, add a wide chisel (1½ in. or so) for paring and chamfering in tight spots. Don't be afraid to start with a

COPING SAW

SHOULDER PLANE

CHISELS

less expensive set. You may need to sharpen a little more often, but that's always good practice and you'll be less afraid of messing things up than you would be if you'd spent a car payment on a top-quality set.

There's no need to be precious about getting rid of the waste between pins and tails, so I initially use a COPING SAW to do it before paring to the baseline with a chisel. You will save a huge amount of time compared to chopping away all of the waste with a chisel. In addition to cutting fast, coping saws also turn on a dime—perfect for maneuvering between pins or tails—and the cheap, replaceable blades mean you can always have a sharp one ready. Its close relative, the fretsaw, is really handy to have as well (see p. 75). On thinner stock, you can slide the thin blade right down the sawkerf of a dovetail and saw along the baseline, leaving just a thin line of waste to chop away. A fretsaw gets overpowered by hardwoods and thicker boards, so don't buy one instead of a coping saw, but plan on adding it at some time.

Regardless of how you cut joinery, you should have a SHOULDER PLANE, because nothing is better for fine-tuning joints for a perfect fit. What makes this plane unique is that the blade extends the full width of the sole, so you can plane right into a corner. If you try to plane a tenon cheek with a block plane, you'll end up with a tapered tenon. Shoulder planes come in a range of widths, from ½ in. to 1¼ in., but I find a wider plane is more versatile, handling broad tenon cheeks as well as narrow shoulders. It also has a lot of mass, which helps it stay flat on its sole and move with force when making cross-grain cuts.

TOOLS FOR SHAPING AND SMOOTHING

The flat surfaces and crisp chamfers that handplanes create are impossible to replicate with a sander.

A good finish starts with good surface preparation, and hand tools are the fastest way to remove machine marks and tearout. The flat surfaces and crisp chamfers that handplanes create are impossible to replicate with a sander. A smoother and a block plane are the two planes to have. Add a card scraper to work really difficult grain and a spokeshave for cleaning up curved surfaces.

For chamfering edges, leveling joints, and smoothing end grain, the **BLOCK PLANE** is indispensable. It also is perfect for paring the end grain on dovetails. Block planes are available in standard and low-angle models. I recommend a low-angle plane with an adjustable throat. This allows you to take a fine cut with a small mouth, which helps to prevent tearout.

On woods with tricky grain, like tiger maple, or when you've got a small bit of tearout on an otherwise clean board, there's no tool like a **CARD SCRAPER**. Unlike a handplane, a scraper has no risk of tearout. Even when I handplane a surface, I'll often follow up with a card scraper to remove any imperfections.

The **SPOKESHAVE** is probably the most overlooked tool in the shop. This odd-looking tool is actually a short-soled handplane with handles on the side, rather than in front of and behind the blade. Nothing is faster at smoothing bandsawn curves. The tool is available with a flat or curved sole, but I recommend the flat sole, as it works well even on concave surfaces.

At last we come to that most iconic hand tool, the **SMOOTHING PLANE**. I fared well for many years using only sanders to smooth surfaces, though today I couldn't imagine being without a plane. You can go from machine marks to a glass-smooth surface in just a few swipes. It's that rare instance in woodworking where the most enjoyable path is also the most efficient, and the results are superior to sanding. The size to start with is a No. 4. If you mill all your lumber with machines, you don't really need the flattening ability of a longer plane. The easiest path to making shavings is to buy a good-quality new plane—Lie-Nielsen® and Veritas are proven products. An old plane, like a venerable Stanley Bailey, offers good quality at an initial savings but requires some tune-up work and probably a new replacement blade. Regardless of the plane you buy, it has to be razor sharp. Even the most expensive plane is nothing but a paperweight if it's dull.

SPOKESHAVE

SMOOTHING PLANE

CARD SCRAPER

BLOCK PLANE

GOOD WORK STARTS WITH GETTING SHARP

An unfortunate truth of woodworking is that your tools have to be sharp. A tool will perform in a way consistent with its level of sharpness. OK, nothing new there. But here's the thing: If your tool is always dull, your expectation of the performance of the tool is consistent with how it performs. In other words, if you are used to using a dull tool, you will be happy with a dull tool. "It does what it's supposed to do, so it's sharp enough." So, in a way, it is. (By the way, this is a really important point, because it's a huge roadblock to doing better work.)

I've found that the biggest aid in getting sharp is to hand a woodworker a tool that's sharp to begin with. Once you have a chance to use a sharp tool, the standard of "sharp enough" has just changed. Once you start using sharp tools, you begin to get greedy, in a good way. Because once your tool stops behaving in the way you like, you take the time to get it sharp again. Or you decide you need to learn how to get it sharp to that point. Either way, you are on your way to doing better work.

Woodworking at its core is a subtractive process. We start with a log, reduce it to boards, remove the moisture, and then take those boards and make small parts. Then we groove and notch them until they fit together. Finally, we smooth the surfaces by removing even more material. Almost all of the mistakes we make during this process involve taking off too much material, causing loose-fitting joints or tearout.

Just about every tool we use works by removing material in a controlled manner. The sharper the tools, the better they can do that. A sharp chisel, for instance, can take a thinner cut than a dull one. And the thickness of the cut determines the level of accuracy you can work to. A dull chisel taking heavy cuts will get you from too tight to too loose really fast. A sharp chisel taking a thin shaving offers a much greater level of precision and a chance to sneak up on a fit. The same is true with a handplane, in a slightly different way. The nemesis of a handplaned surface is tearout. And tearout is directly related to the thickness of a cut you take. The sharper you are, the thinner the cut you can take. And the thinner the cut, the less tearout you'll get.

SO WHAT'S IT TAKE TO GET SHARP?

A sharp edge is often described as the intersection of two flat and polished planes. What this means is that we need to work on the back of the blade as well as the front. The approach to sharpening can vary a little from tool to tool, so the best place to begin is with the chisel. Once you learn how to get your chisels sharp, you'll know 90% of what you need to know about getting sharp. You'll handle your block plane, shoulder plane, and spokeshave blades in the same way. You'll want to take an extra step with your smoothing plane, however. While the other tools benefit from a flat bevel, a slight crown on a plane used for smoothing surfaces will keep the corners from digging in and creating plane tracks.

Regardless of the tool, flattening the back is always the first step. Depending on the quality and condition of the tool, this can take some time and elbow grease. The good news is that it's a one-time effort.

My sharpening kit consists of waterstones in three grits—1,000, 4,000, and 8,000—as well as an inexpensive honing guide. With them, I can get sharp in just a few minutes.

Once you start using sharp tools, you begin to get greedy, in a good way. Because once your tool stops behaving in the way you like, you take the time to get it sharp again.

A BASIC SHARPENING KIT

A pair of Norton combination stones is an inexpensive way to get started with waterstones (1). In addition, I recommend using a honing guide. Inexpensive side-clamping guides are readily available (2), while better quality guides are available from Veritas and Lie-Nielsen. Once you dial in the angle you want, make a set-up block to get you back there easily (3).

SHARPENING A CHISEL

Begin by flattening the back of the chisel. Start on the 4,000-grit stone, working across the surface of the stone to keep from dishing it out (**1**). Only the area adjacent to the edge of the chisel needs to be polished, so don't waste time trying to polish the entire back. Rest just an inch or so of the blade on the stone and keep it dead-flat to the stone as you polish. When the back shows an even scratch pattern (**2**), repeat the process on the 8,000-grit stone for a final polish.

I recommend using a honing guide when working on the bevel. Mount the chisel at 35° and start on the 1,000-grit stone, working on the backstroke (**3**) to avoid gouging the stone. Once you have a continuous line of polish (**4**), move progressively through the finer grits, finishing on the 8,000-grit stone.

Finally, flip the chisel and polish the back on the 8,000-grit stone to remove any burr caused by working the bevel (**5**). Paring the end grain on a piece of pine is a good test to see how sharp you are (**6**). A thin shaving and a glass-smooth surface mean you've done well.

A SHARP CHISEL WILL TREAT YOU WELL

A chisel is a good friend to have. It's the closest thing to a pocket knife or utility tool in your tool kit. Its simple geometry, a flat back with a beveled face, is the key to its effectiveness. You should be able to lay a chisel flat and pare a pin flush with a surface, and it should be able to find a fine scribe line better than your eyes can. To accomplish both of these tasks, the chisel has to be sharp and sharpened in the right way. A quick look at someone's ½-in. chisel and I can tell a lot about the woodwork they are doing, whether they're struggling or they're having fun getting the job done. A chisel isn't a difficult tool to sharpen. In fact, the longer you spend doing it, the less likely that you're getting the results you want. With a tool in good condition, it shouldn't take longer than a couple of minutes to get sharp and to get back to work. A flat and polished back is the key to good performance as well as getting the chisel sharp. Tackle the job once on a tool and you'll never have do it again. From there, all you need to do is to hone the leading edge of the bevel and you're making shavings again.

5

6

GETTING YOUR BEVEL BACK

The honed portion of the bevel will eventually get too wide and you'll be removing too much steel when you sharpen (above). At this point, you'll need to re-establish the primary bevel (bottom). There are a few ways of doing this, and all have their advantages and drawbacks.

The least expensive option is to set your blade in a honing guide at the original bevel angle and run it over 100-grit sandpaper glued to a flat surface. This yields an accurate bevel without the risk of overheating (or "bluing") the steel but is the slowest option.

Next is a high-speed grinder. It's fast, but it can be difficult to grind a clean, consistent bevel. You also run the risk of overheating the steel.

The third option is a slow-speed wet wheel grinder (inset). This is what I've had in my shop for quite a while. It creates a con-

sistent bevel with no risk of bluing. Unfortunately, it's also the most expensive option. So pick your poison and assess your priorities when it comes to grinding.

SHARPENING A PLANE IRON

There's a fine line between a plane that leaves a glass-smooth surface and one that leaves a trail of tearout in its wake.

Of all my hand tools, I take the most care in getting my smoothing planes sharp. There's a fine line between a plane that leaves a glass-smooth surface and one that leaves a trail of tearout in its wake. It's the reason I caution woodworkers from jumping right into working with a handplane before getting set up with a good sharpening routine. That said, getting sharp enough to do good work isn't a particular challenge once you know what you're after. The process is similar to sharpening a chisel, but adding a camber will make all the difference in the world.

Sharpening still begins with polishing the back of the iron, but you can take a short cut here if you wish. Try flattening on the 4,000-grit stone first. If that works quickly and yields an even scratch pattern, just move onto your finest stone. If it looks as though it will take a lot of work, you can use the ruler trick (below) to save a lot of time and wear on your stones.

Once the back is flat, start honing the bevel on the coarse stone as you would a chisel, but introduce a slight camber to the blade with your medium and fine stones. This is a task that would be difficult, if not impossible, to do by hand, but a honing guide lets you do it with ease. Just a little extra pressure here and there, and you've got it.

THE RULER TRICK

It can be difficult to flatten a wide plane iron, but you can speed the process with the help of a thin ruler. Place the ruler along the edge of the 8,000-grit stone (**1**) and rest the blade on it when honing (**2**). Lifting the blade slightly allows you to polish just the leading edge (**3**), which saves a lot of time and wear on your waterstones. New, high-quality blades may not need it, so try them out flat on your 4,000-grit stone. If you get an even scratch pattern quickly, you can skip the ruler.

ADDING A CAMBER TO A PLANE IRON

I like to add a slight camber to planes I use for final smoothing in order to avoid plane tracks caused by the corners cutting into the surface. A honing guide makes the process simple. Start by honing a flat bevel on the 1,000-grit stone and then add the camber on the 4,000-grit stone. Hone with even pressure at first to remove the scratches left by the coarse stone. Then take a few more passes, pressuring first one side of the blade (**1**) and then the other (**2**). Don't lift the blade off the stone, but just change pressure from one side to the other, which is enough to create a slight crown to the blade. Repeat the process on the 8,000-grit stone.

Sometimes you can see a slight arch to the honed edge (**3**), but you won't really know if you have too much or too little camber until you use the blade. If you start taking very narrow shavings and have to extend the blade to get a full-width shaving, there's too much camber and you'll end up taking too heavy of a cut. If it's difficult to keep one corner or the other from contacting the wood, there's not enough camber. Adjust your technique accordingly the next time around and it won't be long before you dial in just the right amount where you're taking thin, almost full-width shavings and leaving a mirror finish behind (**4**).

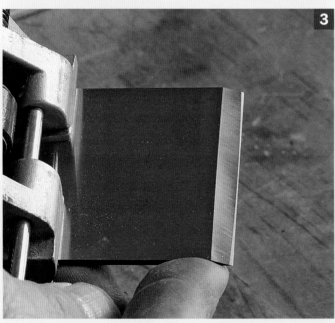

OVERCOMING THE STRESS
OF EXPECTATION

If you don't think you can do the job with the tool at hand, you probably won't. And then the whole notion of the joy of using hand tools is so much hot air.

About the only real skill involved in cutting a dovetail is the ability to start a saw cut where you want it and then cut relatively straight for a short distance. When my students run into trouble, it's not because they can't do that, but because they're not confident that they can. Basically, the expectation is that they are going to screw it up, so a lot of bad things happen after that. First, the muscles get tight, and the knuckles go white from a death grip on the saw. Then the students begin to hedge their bets, either starting away from the line and sawing, or starting at the line but angling away from it once they get going. Not only are they moving away from success, but they're not having fun doing it either. This is the stress of expectation. If you don't think you can do the job with the tool at hand, you probably won't. And then the whole notion of the joy of using hand tools is so much hot air.

I have some simple exercises that get students comfortable with hand tools, and while they do afford the opportunity to build some aptitude, the real aim is to build the confidence that the tool will do what you hope it will do. The first exercise is to draw out vertical lines on a board and saw to them. At first, students are surprised and delighted when they nail a line. But after a while they begin to build the expectation that they will hit the line, until eventually, they will be upset when they miss it. And that's the place to begin. When you pick up a handsaw with the expectation of hitting your line, a lot of good things begin to happen. First, you'll have the confidence to start on your mark, and once you get going, you'll have the confidence to stay on track without the fear of cutting into the good stuff. And once that happens, the joints start fitting faster and tighter, and, last but not least, you start to have fun doing it.

Acquiring competence and comfort with using hand tools is not a long or grueling process. A basic understanding of how the tool works and a little practice will get you going in the right direction. At the heart of the matter are four tools: the backsaw, chisel, block plane, and smoothing plane. Let's throw in a card scraper as well. Mastery of these tools is the foundation for doing good work.

LEARN TO TRUST YOUR BACKSAW

The point is to team up your body with the saw. Neither one of you is perfect, but together you can make perfect cuts.

To cut accurate joinery, you must be able to saw to a line scribed or drawn on a board. The easiest way to become proficient at this is to learn to cut straight down. Then it is just a matter of orienting the workpiece so that the intended line of cut is perpendicular to the benchtop. Simple enough. Even dovetails can be cut in this fashion simply by angling the board in the vise.

The following exercise will help you determine the proper stance for straight cuts. Grab a board and draw a series of lines about 2 in. long, spaced about ¼ in. apart, along the top edge. Pick a line and begin cutting, but don't worry where the saw is heading.

Sawing a straight line depends on setting up properly before you start the cut, then relaxing and letting the saw do the work. Once you start to cut, the saw will end up where you first aimed. Minor course corrections can be made, but blatant attempts at changing direction will wedge the blade in the kerf. Stop after a few cuts and check your progress. The kerfs probably will be off angle a bit. This drift may be due to your stance or to the way the saw was sharpened. Adjusting your stance is the best way to alter the line of cut. If the saw is cutting to the right, move slightly to the right; if it cuts to the left, move to the left. The point is to team up your body with the saw. Neither one of you is perfect, but together you can make perfect cuts.

Start with a good foundation. Move your saw foot back to create a wide stable stance, and place your opposite hand on the bench when sawing to lock your body in position (left). Extend your finger along the saw handle to help align your arm with the saw. Finally, position your shoulder over the saw so everything is in alignment (above).

GET CONFIDENT WITH YOUR SAW

For square cuts, begin with a square setup. Clamp a board in the vise using a square for alignment. Then use the square to draw lines on the board's face (**1**). With plumb lines as a guide, you're ready to start sawing.

Don't worry about staying on the line at first. Try to make full-depth cuts without the saw binding. Once you can do so consistently, you can refine the direction of the cuts with small adjustments in stance until the sawcut hits the line (**2**).

To take it a step further, tape the end grain of a board and scribe lines every ¼ in. or so with a knife. Peel away every other piece and practice starting your sawcut on each side of the pieces of tape that remain (**3**). Once you get confident that you'll cut a straight line and you become comfortable starting right next to a scribe line (**4**), you've pretty much nailed the backsaw and you're ready to cut joinery.

PARING BY HAND

When paring by hand, it's important to get your mass behind the tool. With the work clamped in a vise, assume a wide low stance (1). Take a two-handed grip to lock your upper body into a single unit and use your hips and legs to power the chisel. Gripping the blade near the tip makes it easy to position the chisel exactly where you want it. Use your rear hand to drive the tool into the cut. When paring end grain, saw out most of the waste so you can start paring right at the scribe line (2). If the waste is still too thick, slice a portion away at a time, working across the base line.

Paring along the grain can be a little tricky, depending on how the grain is running. If it's straight or angled out, paring down works well (3). But if the grain is angled into the pin wall, the only option is to pare across the grain (4).

CHISELS: GO THIN TO STAY SHARP

My aim is to remove as much waste as possible before I even pick up a chisel.

A lot of woodworkers I talk to aren't that happy with their chisels. The common complaint: "They just don't hold an edge like I thought they would." The problem is often not the chisels themselves, but how they are being used. In short, the chisel is a tool designed to take a thin shaving. When you take heavy cuts, a chisel dulls quickly. But if you stick to thin cuts, the tool will perform wonderfully and stay sharp for a long time.

My aim is to remove as much waste as possible before I even pick up a chisel. Depending on the joint, I go about this in a few different ways. For dovetails and tenons, I can usually saw out the waste, leaving only 1/32 in. to 1/16 in. remaining to chisel away. When I can't saw it out, I turn to the drill. For mortises, I can drill out the majority of waste before chopping to the knife lines. On half-blind dovetails, drill a row along the baseline while staying clear of the line by 1/32 in. to 1/16 in. There's no need to drill out all of the waste. Once the long-grain fibers are severed, the majority of the waste pops out easily.

Once you do pick up a chisel, there are two ways you can go about it. For fine work, paring by hand offers the most control (above), but for heavier cuts, a hammer or mallet can get you to the finish line faster (p. 64).

When working on a bench, get your shoulder over the tool to provide the driving force. Again, use your leading hand to guide the cut and drive with your rear hand. Work back to the baseline, taking thin cuts until there's just a thin line of waste left before setting the chisel into the scribe line.

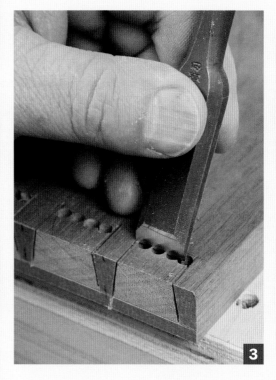

TECHNIQUES FOR CHOPPING

With a hammer or mallet providing the power, the key is controlling the chisel. Rather than gripping the handle, hold the blade near the tip. Pinch the blade between your thumb and fingers and rest your hand on the surface of the workpiece (**1**). This low grip lets you place the chisel more accurately and allows your chisel hand to act as a brake to keep the chisel from exiting the workpiece and contacting the benchtop.

Just as when paring by hand, take thin cuts. Work toward the baseline until you're within 1/32 in. Then place the chisel right in the scribe line and angle it slightly forward for the final chop (**2**). This purposeful undercut helps the joint seat tightly, but you must stop halfway through the cut, flip the workpiece, and finish chopping from the baseline on the opposite side.

On half-blind dovetails, drill a row of holes to sever as much of the end grain as possible before chopping. Start chopping at the widest part of the holes (**3**) and pop out the waste with a horizontal chop (**4**). Continue working toward the baseline (**5**) until just a sliver remains, and then place the chisel in the scribe line for a final cut (**6**).

Working this way, you'll be surprised at how little force is needed and how controlled and precise the process is.

4

5 6

MORTISES: END GRAIN FIRST

Drill out as much of the waste as you can before picking up a chisel. After that, the first task is always to establish the end-grain walls of the mortise (above). These fibers are much tougher to cut than the long-grain fibers on the sides of the mortise. Once the ends are established, start at the center of the mortise and work toward the scribe lines, taking thin cuts. The waste between the holes is a good indicator that you're paring straight (right).

TACKLE CORNERS WITH A BLOCK PLANE

M y 4-year-old daughter would pay a visit to the shop on occasion. Her activities usually were limited to nailing and gluing scraps together, but when she would see me pick up a block plane to knock an edge off a board, she'd run over to tackle the task herself. Clearly, the block plane is not difficult to use, but you can get better performance from it by practicing a few maneuvers.

I use a block plane chiefly for chamfering the edges of boards. My aim is to cut a 45° chamfer of a consistent depth along the length of the board. To get the hang of this, scribe pencil lines ⅛ in. from both sides of a board's corner. Practice chamfering until you hit the lines. For wide chamfers, I still make it a habit to use layout lines, but for anything less than ¼ in. wide, I rely on technique and let my eye be the judge.

CONSISTENT CHAMFERS

Planing consistent chamfers is a skill you'll use often, so it's important to get the hang of it early on. Guidelines on each face make a good target for checking your progress as you dial in your technique. Use a combination square to pencil lines roughly ⅛ in. from the edge and face of the board (**1**).

To cut the chamfer, start with the blade set for a fairly heavy cut and make sure you're heading in the direction of the grain. The key to a consistent chamfer is to start with just the front section of the plane in contact with the wood (**2**). The idea is to start taking a shaving right at the corner. If not, you'll end up with a tapered chamfer.

Take a few more passes and check your progress (**3**). If you're getting closer to one line than the other, try to correct the angle of the plane before you get too close to the lines. You want to end up with a single facet that's consistent in width along its length and hits each pencil line. The benefit of making the effort is subtle but important. A clean chamfer will create a sharp, consistent highlight when the light strikes your work and will add to the crispness of the overall piece.

CHIP-FREE END GRAIN

When chamfering the ends of a board, the aim is to avoid tearout at the corners. Working in the correct direction and angling the plane can both help to prevent it. To get started, use a marking gauge to scribe a ⅛-in. shoulder around one end of a board and along each edge of the end grain. On an actual workpiece, I'd use a pencil if anything at all, because the cuts from the marking gauge will remain after the chamfer is complete. In this case, the scribe lines are there to provide a better target as you practice chamfering all four edges of the end of a board.

Clamp the board securely in a vise and chamfer the first end (**1**). Skew the block plane and cut from the base toward the top. The finished chamfer should be a single facet that hits each scribe line. Turn the board and chamfer the other end. By chamfering the ends first, you'll avoid tearout as you plane the sides. When the ends are done, start chamfering the long edges (**2**), trying to hit the scribe lines evenly on the final pass. To prevent tearout, skew the plane as you move it parallel to the edge. As you finish the chamfer, don't let the side bevel become deeper than the end bevel, or you can end up with tearout. All the chamfers should meet exactly at the corners (**3**).

Now, flip the board and repeat the exercise on the other end, this time without the scribe lines. The result may not be perfect, but if you concentrate on clean bevels that align at the corners, it should look pretty nice without a lot of time spent scribing lines.

A SHARP BLADE AND LIGHT CUTS

The whole idea of getting sharp is to be able to take a thin cut. If you start out too heavy, you've thrown all of that hard work away. To set up the blade, first retract it fully into the sole. Then advance it slowly, feeling for the blade with a finger at each corner (1). If you start to feel one corner emerge first, tilt the lateral adjuster toward that high corner until the blade is level with the sole (2). Then extend the blade until you can just feel it with both fingers. It probably won't cut yet, but it's a good place to start.

Take a few passes on a board, slowly adjusting the depth of cut until you take a whisper of a shaving. Check to see if it's centered on the blade; if not, hit the lateral adjuster again until the shaving is centered. You can now extend the blade just a hint farther and get to work. Don't worry if the shavings are hit and miss at first. As the board flattens, you should begin to take full shavings (3). With a properly cambered blade, you should be able to take a thin shaving that's almost the full width of the blade (4). Skewing the plane as you work creates a slicing motion and helps to prevent the blade from chattering.

If you're planing in the right direction and still getting tearout, take a look at your shavings (5). They should be light and fluffy and squish when you squeeze them. If they crinkle like dry leaves, the cut is too heavy, which is probably the reason for the tearout.

PUT YOUR HANDPLANE TO WORK

A smoothing plane isn't absolutely necessary for woodworking, but nothing beats one for quickly removing machine marks, leaving a surface ready for finishing.

Most woodworkers I know have had a bad experience with a handplane, and I'm no exception. After an early run-in with a dull handplane, I gave up on planes and resigned myself to a lot of sanding. It wasn't until years later, when I was handed a sharp, well-tuned smoothing plane, that I finally discovered the joy of taking a paper-thin shaving off the edge of a board. A smoothing plane isn't absolutely necessary for woodworking, but nothing beats one for quickly removing machine marks, leaving a surface ready for finishing (or just a few swipes of fine sandpaper away from it).

Of all the tools mentioned so far, sharpness is most critical to the performance of a handplane. The sharper the blade, the thinner the shaving you can take, and the better the resulting surface.

The two basic jobs of a smoothing plane are jointing (making the edge of a board straight and square to its sides) and smoothing the face of a board. The first key to success is getting the blade set for a light cut and level with the sole. After that, learn the proper weight shift from the front of the plane to the rear as you make a pass, and you'll be taking nice shavings.

FIND THE BALANCE

Effective planing involves a gradual weight shift from front to back during a pass while keeping the plane's sole flat on the board. Here's a quick exercise that lets you get a feel for this concept. Take a 6-in.-wide board and stand it on edge. Place the front end against a stop and take some full-length passes. Doing so without the board tipping over or lifting off the bench requires that you shift your weight as you go and stay centered over the board. After a while this will become second nature.

THE CARD SCRAPER IS A LIFESAVER

What a card scraper lacks in sex appeal it makes up for in ease of setup and use with no risk of tearout.

When you think of working with hand tools, the humble card scraper is probably not the first tool to come to mind. But what it lacks in sex appeal it makes up for in ease of setup and use with no risk of tearout. Whether or not you use a handplane, the scraper is still a must-have tool for dealing with any tearout from the planer or jointer and for tricky grain that a handplane can't handle. Even though you might be itching to get a handplane going, start here. Using a scraper is simple—the trick is to get it honed properly.

What transforms this piece of steel into a tool is the hook on its edge, often mistakenly referred to as a "burr." Creating the hook is the key to good performance, but a few common missteps when burnishing the hook prevent most woodworkers from getting the best out of their scrapers. In short, when turning the hook, keep the pressure light to avoid crimping the steel and the angle low to let the scraper work more aggressively.

THE HOOK IS THE KEY

Before you burnish the scraper, you need to polish the faces and edges. I use a DMT® fine/extra-fine combination diamond plate, but sandpaper would work just as well. Start with 400-grit and finish with 600-grit.

Work the faces as you would the back of a chisel or plane iron, and then move on to the edges. The first step is to file them square. On a scraper that's been used, this is especially important. Slip the scraper into a block with a sawkerf and clamp it in a vise (1). Extending the scraper just a little helps to ensure that you're filing square (2).

To smooth the filed edge, head back to the diamond plate or sandpaper (3). At this point, there's probably a slight burr remaining along the corner. To remove it, alternate between polishing the face and the edge. The result should be a smooth, sharp corner.

To create the hook, start by laying the scraper flat and drawing out the steel. Keep the burnisher flat, but apply pressure over the edge and angle it to draw the steel away from the edge (4). To turn the hook, place the scraper back in the block with ⅛ in. protruding. Tilt the burnisher 1 or 2 degrees and take a couple of light passes (5). Two swipes on each corner are all you need. The resulting hook is small and you might think it would take just a light shaving, but it can be as aggressive as you'd like it to be.

When the edge dulls, just draw the edge back up and turn the hook again. It lasts longer the second and third time you turn it, because the steel gets progressively harder. But eventually the steel becomes brittle, and it's necessary to file off the edge and start again.

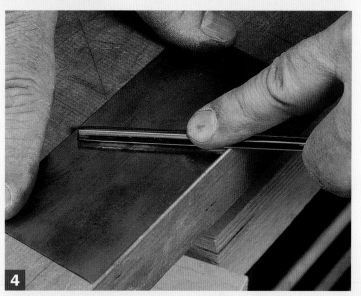

PUT IT ALL TOGETHER AND CUT A DOVETAIL

The dovetail is not a difficult joint to cut. Nevertheless, it's a stress-inducing thing for a lot of woodworkers.

Now let's take a few minutes and cut a dovetail. If you've given the hand-tool exercises a try, then you're pretty much already there. Dovetails show up quite a bit, and it's a useful joint to know—and not a difficult joint to cut. Nevertheless, it's a stress-inducing thing for a lot of woodworkers. That's probably the sole reason that a dovetail router jig market even exists, because nothing could be worse than setting up one of those. So, if the fear of cutting a dovetail by hand is such that it may lead you to that extreme, let's get it out of the way now.

When I was first learning to play the guitar, the F-chord was my nemesis. It was such a challenge that I tended to avoid songs where it appeared. And when there was no choice but to play it, my attention throughout the song was focused on that point where it showed up. Needless to say, the joy of playing was severely compromised because of it. If the dovetail is your F-chord, the sooner you get comfortable with it the more you'll really begin to enjoy the craft. A while back, someone commented that I must enjoy cutting dovetails because they appear so often in my work. The truth of the matter is that I don't really give them any thought; if the joint is important for the melody of a particular piece, I simply play it along with all of the other notes.

The biggest dovetail worry seems to involve sawing, but all you're really doing is cutting a relatively straight line for a short distance with a backsaw. Once you master that, which won't take long, the real challenge is to get your layout marks in the right place, because even if you hit your line, you'll still end up with a headache if it's not where it should be. So most of my tips have to do with layout.

STEP 1: TAILS

Though many woodworkers start by cutting the pins, I always start with the tails. For me, it's the fastest and most accurate method. (My tips for cutting dovetails are specific to this approach, so if you cut the pins first and are happy with your progress, skip ahead. On the other hand, you might want to stick around for the conversation. You never know . . . .)

Before we can get to cutting the tails, we need to scribe a baseline on all of the parts with a marking gauge (**1**). When the dovetails will be flush to the surface, on drawer sides for instance, set the gauge to the thickness of the stock. When you want them to stick out a bit, set the gauge slightly wider than the stock.

The dovetail angle is usually described as a ratio, often 1:6 for softwoods or 1:8 for hardwoods. I like the look of the more slender 1:8 tails, so I go with that ratio all of the time. The spacing of the tails is more an aesthetic concern, but I try to get them visually even. For the most part, I space them by eye, but for exposed dovetails on case work, I tend to measure them out. Make a tick mark at each pin location and pencil in the angled sides using a bevel gauge (**2**).

When cutting the tails, exactly where you start and what angle you cut at aren't important enough to stress about. Yes, aim to hit your line, but don't worry about it (**3**). The important thing is to saw square to the face of the stock; this will have a big impact on how easy it is to fit the joint later.

Clear out most of the waste before chopping to the baseline. A coping saw is great for thick stock and hardwoods, but I like to use a fretsaw when I can. Its thin blade can slip down the backsaw kerf, which lets you saw straight across the baseline, leaving just a little waste to chisel away (**4**). Then saw off the waste from the edges (**5**). To remove the waste, chop in halfway from each face (**6**). This will create a slight undercut that will guarantee that nothing will hold up the joint.

When cutting the tails, exactly where you start and what angle you cut at aren't important enough to stress about. Yes, aim to hit your line, but don't worry about it.

STEP 2: SCRIBING

With the tails cut we can get down to work. The next step, transferring the tail locations to the pin board, is the most critical. I'm not really a gadget kind of person, but I have a couple of aids that will make sure the layout marks are where they need to be.

Start by laying down a strip of blue painter's tape on the end grain of the pin board (**1**). Be sure to trim the tape with a knife (**2**), rather than folding it over the edge. After knifing the lines, you'll peel away the tape from the waste areas for a clear roadmap for sawing. This simple technique has worked wonders not just on my dovetails but on my students' dovetails as well. Give it a try.

When scribing the lines, it's important that the tail board doesn't shift during the process. If it does, the lines will end up in the wrong place. To make positioning the parts easier, I use a support block with a lip that makes it a snap to set the height of the pin board above the benchtop (**3**). The block is square in cross-section with a ¼-in.-thick strip of wood glued to one face to create the lip.

In addition to the block, I clamp a jig along the base of the tails to help with alignment. The tail board has to be accurately positioned in three different aspects. It has to be square to the pin board, aligned side to side, and located accurately front to back for the joint to fit properly. The jig handles all of these tasks. It consists of a small rectangle of ¼-in. MDF, with a slotted piece of pine glued along one edge. The ends of the pine fence should extend past the MDF.

To use the jig, align it to the tails and secure with a spring clamp (**4**). Register the edge of the jig against the pin board and slide it side to side until the fence is flush against one end. The jig can still shift if you're not careful, so use a light touch. Press down on the tail board midway between the pin board and the support block to hold it securely in place for scribing (**5**). Knife along each tail wall and check that your scribe lines are tight against the stock. Peel away the tape from the waste areas to make it clear where to saw (**6**). Then pencil a vertical line down from each scribe line (**7**) as a visual aid for sawing and when paring the joint later.

1

STEP 3: PINS

When sawing the pins, try to start your cuts adjacent to the tape (1). Make a few light strokes to establish a kerf, then reset your position for finishing the cut. This is really important when sawing on the left side of the pins, because you have to lean over the saw to see where you're cutting. If you maintain that position while cutting, your line is likely to wander off your mark. So instead, peek over the saw to start the cut, and then resume a normal posture for the rest of the cut. You won't be able to see what the saw is doing, but you don't need to once the kerf is established. This is one time when trust is an especially good thing.

Cope and chop the waste as before (2 & 3), and then check your fit. Ideally, at least a portion of the joint will seat at this point. The problem with sawing away from the scribe line as a practice is that none of the joint will fit at the start and it can be difficult to know where to pare without creat-

ing gaps in the joint. Before you go too far, check to see if your cuts were vertical and pare any side walls that need it without removing stock from the top edge of the joint. Also, take a look to see if there's any waste remaining between the tape and any of the sawkerfs and pare it away, making sure not to cut into the tape (4). Then check that there's no waste left in the corners of the joint (5)—it doesn't take a lot to keep it from seating.

If you did a good job of aligning the parts for scribing and you sawed or pared to the tape, there's a really good chance the joint will go together (6). If you can get it fully seated across the joint, but it won't go all the way in, pull it apart and run a pencil line along the inside bottom edge of the pin sockets of the tail board. Tap it back in place and remove it to show pencil marks on the pins that need to be pared.

RHYTHM IS AT THE
HEART OF GOOD WORK

Sometimes, if I'm a little stressed about the task at hand and the voices in my head get a little too loud, I'll tell myself to just shut up, relax, and watch the work get done.

When you think of repetitive work, it doesn't sound like such a great thing, but repetition is the key to doing consistent, accurate, fast work—especially when we're talking about handwork.

There's a lot of repetition in handwork, whether it's cutting dovetails or planing parts, and it offers the opportunity to develop efficiencies in our work. I really don't like dovetailing a single drawer. Before I can find my rhythm and stop stressing out about hitting my scribe lines, I'm already finished. Although the drawer typically turns out fine, it doesn't really sing. While tackling seven drawers for a dresser can be a slog, dovetailing two of three drawers can get me in the zone. It forces me to get my parts organized and stacked neatly. As I work, my tools begin to find their natural spot on the bench. Most important, I begin to find the rhythm in each task, and I start to see patterns in the work being done—the number of saw strokes to make a cut, the number of chops to clear the waste. So, after a while, instead of always stopping to check my progress, I begin to trust that the work is getting done. In doing that I find that I begin to work in a state of relaxed concentration.

Sometimes, if I'm a little stressed about the task at hand and the voices in my head get a little too loud, I'll tell myself to just shut up, relax, and watch the work get done. In doing so, I realize that the talky part of the brain, the part that always seems to be driving the bus, is actually counterproductive to getting the results I want. I begin to realize that, wow, I know what I'm doing without stressing about it.

Investing rhythm into our work has a big effect not just on the concrete results of our tasks, but on the overall sense of the piece as well. At first our focus is on getting sharp and comfortable with our tools, and then getting the steps of the process down. After that the challenge is to find the rhythm that turns those actions into a continuous dance. That's when good work truly begins.

CHAPTER 4

CABINETS

The wall cabinet is one of my favorite projects to build and one of my favorite classes to teach. It's not the most basic form, but it contains so much of the DNA that's in just about any project you'll want to tackle in the future. It's a great lesson in case construction and a perfect way to explore different door, drawer, and shelf combinations. The design possibilities are endless, and you can get a lot of woodworking in without going through a lot of lumber. From dovetailed case joinery to through-tenons to a frame-and-panel door and traditional dovetailed drawer construction, a wall cabinet can contain as much as 90% of the basic skills that go into furniture making. From here, it's just about how you want to dress things up.

While a cabinet is a great canvas for exploring ideas, its versatility is also the key to its utility. You can size a cabinet to fit just about any bare patch of wall in a house and transform an unused space into the focal point of a room. You can customize a cabinet to fit almost any contents you can think of and provide valuable storage space where it's needed most.

WALL CABINET NO. 1

With this little cabinet, I began a 10-year journey toward finding a more personal style and building work with a quiet resonance and lasting permanence. It's a path I'm still treading and one I hope to be on for quite a while. So I figured it was a good place to start this chapter. It was a quick project to build, with no major investment of thought, just dovetails at the corners and through-tenons for the shelves. I used up some scraps for the case and raided my stash of ebony for the pulls. I left the dovetails and tenons proud and offset the parts where they met. In spite of its simplicity, something resonated about it. In a way, it was a non-designed piece, so rather than aspiring to be something, it just kind of was.

Shortly before making the cabinet, I had put together a portfolio of my more recent work, which was a mixture of Shaker and Arts and Crafts pieces with a couple of other odds and ends thrown in. I was relatively happy with each piece, but when I saw them as a whole I was struck by the thought that there wasn't really any voice there. There was an anonymity to the collection, some this and that. It wasn't as simple as not having an identifiable style, more that the work didn't connect with what drove my passion as a furniture maker. At the time, I didn't have an idea of how to move forward from there, so I put the thought aside.

But with this simple cabinet, a piece that wasn't "anything," I caught a glimpse of the woodworker I strove to be. And that glimpse gave me a direction forward, leading to a path I've been on for a number of years now. So what is that path, if it isn't about conscious design? Foremost, it's having faith in the notion that making simple work can be enough. My aim isn't a conscious minimalism or austerity, but simply to refrain from making something more than it should be.

It took a while (OK, a long time) to accept the humility that is bound up with the craft of woodworking: The notion that what we build is not an end in itself, not an object to be admired in a vacuum or to be placed on a pedestal, but that it has to be something that works for a living. I don't expect my furniture to be the star of the show or to shout to draw attention to itself, but I do expect it to do its job well and add a quiet soundtrack to its surroundings.

In spite of its simplicity, something resonated about it. In a way, it was a non-designed piece, so rather than aspiring to be something, it just kind of was.

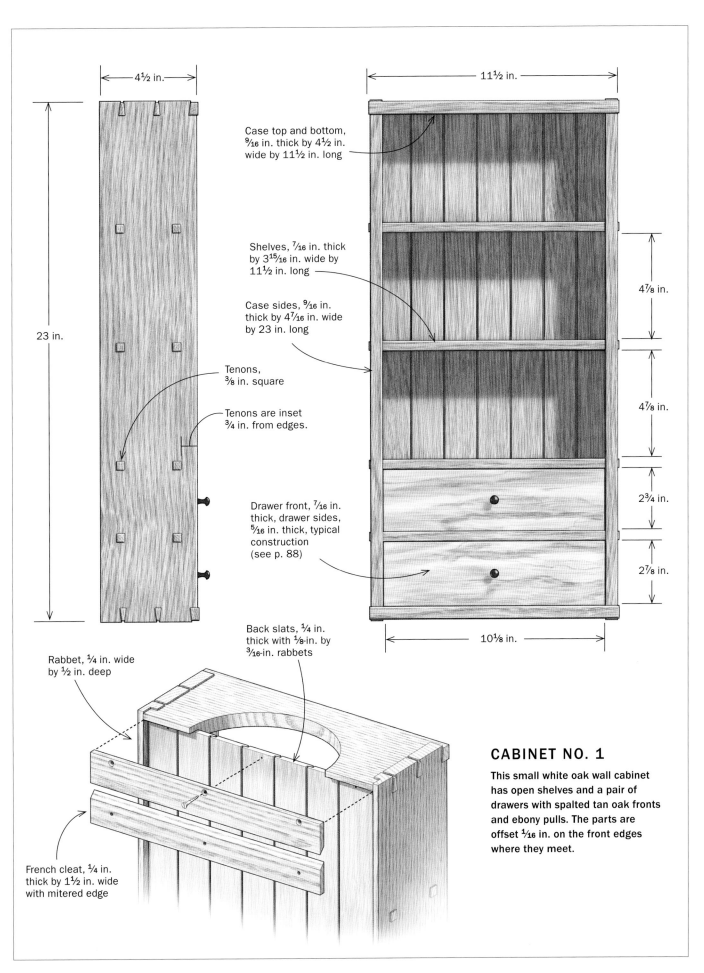

4½ in.

23 in.

Case top and bottom, 9/16 in. thick by 4½ in. wide by 11½ in. long

Shelves, 7/16 in. thick by 3 15/16 in. wide by 11½ in. long

Case sides, 9/16 in. thick by 4 7/16 in. wide by 23 in. long

Tenons, 3/8 in. square

Tenons are inset 3/4 in. from edges.

Drawer front, 7/16 in. thick, drawer sides, 5/16 in. thick, typical construction (see p. 88)

11½ in.

4 7/8 in.

4 7/8 in.

2 3/4 in.

2 7/8 in.

10 1/8 in.

Back slats, 1/4 in. thick with 1/8-in. by 3/16-in. rabbets

Rabbet, 1/4 in. wide by 1/2 in. deep

French cleat, 1/4 in. thick by 1½ in. wide with mitered edge

CABINET NO. 1

This small white oak wall cabinet has open shelves and a pair of drawers with spalted tan oak fronts and ebony pulls. The parts are offset 1/16 in. on the front edges where they meet.

A STUDY IN 1/16s

So here was a dresser built to last a few generations, but it was living out its tenure as an "old" piece of furniture. That bothered me.

As simple as this cabinet is, it still offers a pretty good lesson in design: How an unadorned piece can still have a personality and how a philosophy can drive a multitude of design decisions.

Here's why I call this cabinet a study in 1/16s: Wherever two components meet, they are offset by roughly ¹⁄₁₆ in. And the reason for that dates back to a Shaker dresser I made for my daughter many years ago. One of the key details of that piece was the exposed dovetails along the edges of the case top. I had planed them perfectly flush, but after the first heating season, I could run my hand across them and feel the slight ridges of the joinery. In those slight offsets, the dresser was no longer "perfect," no longer "new." So here was a dresser built to last a few generations, but it was living out its tenure as an "old" piece of furniture. That bothered me. So rather than continue to plane case joinery flush and curse it when it moved, I began to leave the joinery proud of the surface.

Proud joinery is a common detail in Arts and Crafts furniture, which I had been enamored with for years, so it wasn't a big stretch to add it to other work. One of the things I like about Arts and Crafts furniture is that it wears its age well, and part of its staying power has to do with the proud joinery. Whereas a joint that is smoothed flush will eventually move, a joint that is left proud will always be proud.

My intent is to build a piece of furniture that will age gracefully over time. After the finish has faded a bit and life has imparted its patina of dings and scratches, the essence of the piece will still be intact. In a way, I'm working and designing with the acceptance of age and use, and embracing that process rather than resisting it.

I used to think in terms of building furniture that lasted a long time. I now tend to think in terms of building furniture that will have a long life. The difference is subtle but significant. Rather than hope for a piece to survive long enough to be considered an antique, I'd rather build a

(Continued on p. 90)

A SIMPLE WALL CABINET

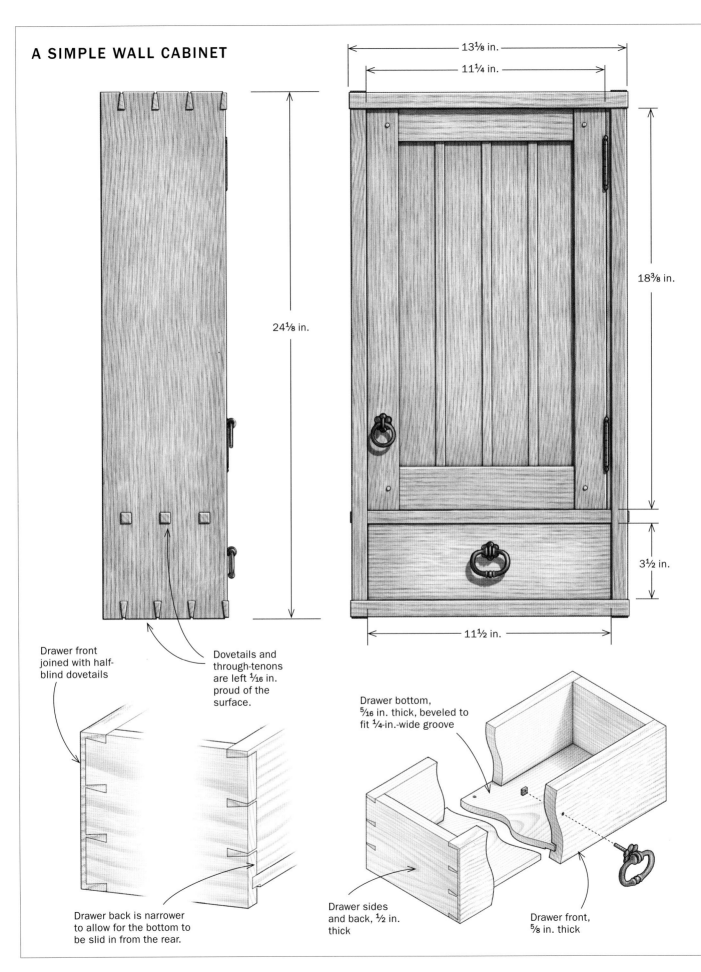

13⅛ in.

11¼ in.

24⅛ in.

18⅜ in.

3½ in.

11½ in.

Drawer front joined with half-blind dovetails

Dovetails and through-tenons are left 1⁄16 in. proud of the surface.

Drawer bottom, 5⁄16 in. thick, beveled to fit ¼-in.-wide groove

Drawer back is narrower to allow for the bottom to be slid in from the rear.

Drawer sides and back, ½ in. thick

Drawer front, 5⁄8 in. thick

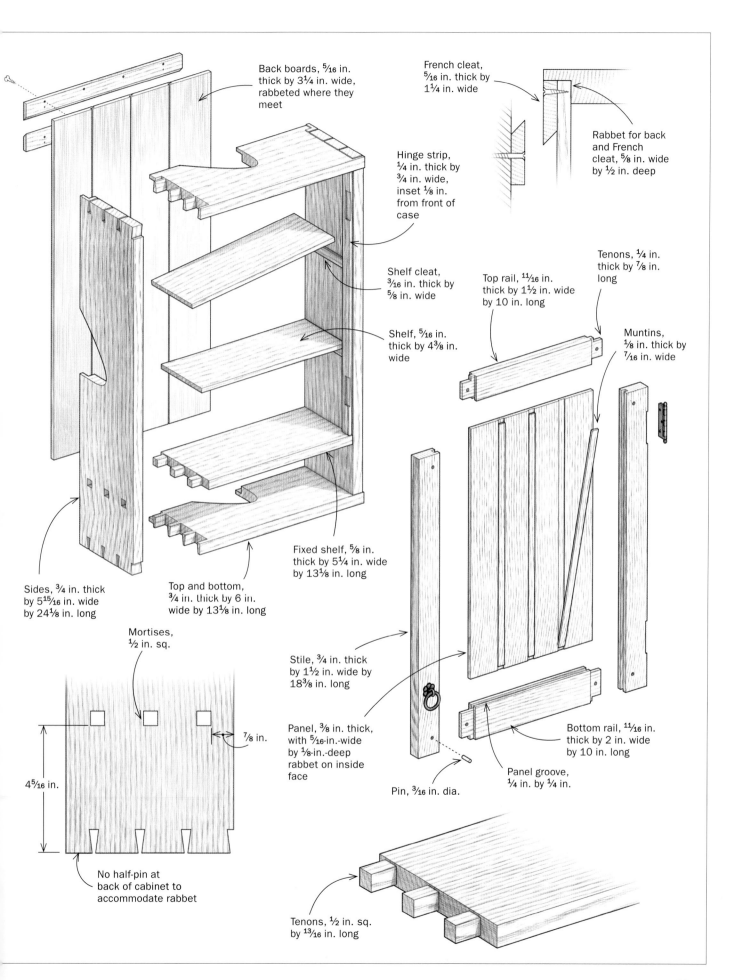

Back boards, ⁵⁄₁₆ in. thick by 3¼ in. wide, rabbeted where they meet

French cleat, ⁵⁄₁₆ in. thick by 1¼ in. wide

Rabbet for back and French cleat, ⁵⁄₈ in. wide by ½ in. deep

Hinge strip, ¼ in. thick by ¾ in. wide, inset ⅛ in. from front of case

Shelf cleat, ³⁄₁₆ in. thick by ⁵⁄₈ in. wide

Shelf, ⁵⁄₁₆ in. thick by 4⅜ in. wide

Top rail, ¹¹⁄₁₆ in. thick by 1½ in. wide by 10 in. long

Tenons, ¼ in. thick by ⅞ in. long

Muntins, ⅛ in. thick by ⁷⁄₁₆ in. wide

Fixed shelf, ⁵⁄₈ in. thick by 5¼ in. wide by 13⅛ in. long

Sides, ¾ in. thick by 5¹⁵⁄₁₆ in. wide by 24⅛ in. long

Top and bottom, ¾ in. thick by 6 in. wide by 13⅛ in. long

Mortises, ½ in. sq.

⁷⁄₈ in.

4⁵⁄₁₆ in.

No half-pin at back of cabinet to accommodate rabbet

Stile, ¾ in. thick by 1½ in. wide by 18⅜ in. long

Panel, ⅜ in. thick, with ⁵⁄₁₆-in.-wide by ⅛-in.-deep rabbet on inside face

Pin, ³⁄₁₆ in. dia.

Panel groove, ¼ in. by ¼ in.

Bottom rail, ¹¹⁄₁₆ in. thick by 2 in. wide by 10 in. long

Tenons, ½ in. sq. by ¹³⁄₁₆ in. long

Fitting doors and drawers is challenge enough, but it can be a nightmare if you're trying to get them into a case that isn't square. While building the case, I stress about gaps in joinery, grain that's not exactly as I'd like, and so on, but if it measures square corner to corner once the clamps are on, all is forgiven.

piece that gets put to use, and then is maybe forgotten and later rediscovered to be put to use again. I like the notion of someone chancing upon a piece at a flea market, a piece with no signature or provenance, and thinking, "Oh, that could work in the entry hall."

So, yes, the joinery in my work tends to stick out a bit. There's another reason for it as well. It's the notion that if you can see two parts come together, your hand should be able to feel them come together as well. This is important, because we experience a piece of furniture not just with our eyes, but also with our hands. We interact with it—we sit in chairs, eat at tables, open doors and drawers—so using a piece of furniture is a tactile as well as a visual experience. It makes sense then that we anticipate the effect on the hand as well as the eye. This is a second philosophy that drives the design of my work.

The other effect of the offsets between parts is the subtle shadows and highlights that are created by them. In the same way that a carving or decorative molding is designed to catch the light, so do these slight "imperfections." A wonderful thing about these offsets is that they can change the nature of a piece by the way the light hits it. A wall cabinet by a window will have a different personality in the morning than it does

(Continued on p. 94)

DOVETAILS WITH A BUILT-IN RABBET

This twist on the traditional dovetail is a great joint for cabinets and eliminates the need to rout a rabbet on the back edge after glue-up. It's not difficult to cut and it's a perfect joint for any cabinet with a rabbeted back.

Start by laying out the tails on the case sides, skipping the half-pin at the back edge. Be sure to leave enough room behind the last pin to cut a rabbet without cutting into the pin. After cutting the tails, cut the rabbet in all of the case parts (**1**), and then scribe the pins on the case top and bottom as you normally would (**2**). I add blue tape to the end grain and use an alignment guide to help get the tail board in the right position. Now cut and chop the pins. You'll be left with a tab at the back corner that will prevent the joint from fully seating. Scribe and cut the tab to length (**3**), sneaking up on the fit until the joint fully seats with no gap at the baseline or at the tab (**4**).

A SPACER BLOCK
FOR THROUGH-TENONS

To prevent gaps, your layout marks must be accurate. The challenge with through-mortises is that the layout has to be in the same location on each face. In addition, the tenons need to match the mortises. To solve that headache (I mean challenge), I lay out the joinery using a spacer block and marking gauge (another example of doing better work by measuring less).

Start by making a spacer block and cut the tenon cheeks to match the spacer (**1**). Now you can lay out the mortises in the case sides and the widths of the tenons with the help of the spacer.

When laying out through-joinery, I first lay down some blue painter's tape over the area of the joint. I scribe through the tape and peel it off the waste areas to give me a clear-cut guide for sawing and chopping.

Pencil in the approximate location of the top and bottom of the mortises on the case sides. You'll dial it in later, but this will provide a starting point and a stopping point for scribing the sides of the mortises.

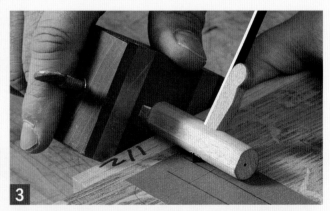

Set the gauge to the inside wall of an outer mortise and scribe each face of both case sides (**2**). Use the same gauge setting to scribe the ends of the shelf tenon. Now, place the spacer block against the edge of the case side, register the gauge against it, and scribe the outside wall of each outer mortise (**3**). Use the spacer to scribe the outside wall of each tenon as well (**4**).

Adjust the gauge to scribe one wall of the center mortise. Scribe it and rotate the workpiece, registering off the opposite edge to scribe the second wall. Repeat for the center tenons on the shelf.

All that's left of the layout is to scribe the tops and bottoms of the mortises. Register the gauge off the bottom of the case and scribe the top of the mortise, and then insert the block to scribe the bottom (**5**). Now peel away the tape from the waste areas. The tough part is over. It's time to cut some joinery.

For the mortises, begin by drilling out most of the waste. Then chisel to the scribe lines, working halfway in from each face (**6**). Use a backsaw to cut the tenon walls. Cope away most of the waste between the tenons and then chisel to the base-line (**7**). Work halfway in from each face, undercutting the joint slightly as you go. This will ensure that there isn't any waste to keep the joint from fully seating (**8**).

HANGING A DOOR

The door to this cabinet is traditional frame-and-panel construction. On this case, I've added vertical muntins to dress up the panel. Before gluing up the door, rip shallow grooves on the face of the panel at each muntin location (**1**). After assembling the door, glue thin strips into the muntin grooves (**2**). Finally, pin the corners of the frame at each joint, leaving the pins ¹⁄₁₆ in. proud of the surface.

On this project, as well as a lot of others, I chose to inset the door from the front of the cabinet. This can be a little tricky, but a hinge strip solves the problem. Rather than mortise the case side for the door hinges, I mortise a thin strip for the hinges and attach it to the inside face of the case side (**3**). It's easier to mortise the strip than the case and I can determine the inset of the door by the placement of the strip. Before installing the hinge strip, scrape the shellac off the case side where the strip will attach. Add a thin bead of glue to the strip and align it to the front edge of the case with a combination square (**4**). To keep the strip from shifting during clamping, I like to tack it in place with a 23-gauge pin at each hinge location. After the door is trimmed to fit the case, shim it so that it is centered vertically and transfer the hinge mortise locations from the hinge strip to the door (**5**).

When building the cabinet, the key is coming up with a strategy for creating the offsets that doesn't complicate the construction.

in the evening, and a different personality in the hard winter light of February than in the soft shadows of August. It becomes a living thing, a clock, a sundial, a calendar.

When building the cabinet, the key is coming up with a strategy for creating the offsets that doesn't complicate the construction. Some of the offsets are created when cutting the joinery, whereas others are made while trimming parts after the joinery has been cut. The proud joinery is simply a function of a marking gauge set wider than the thickness of the stock. The wider the gauge, the more the joinery will stick out. In my work, I typically set the gauge ¹⁄₁₆ in. wider than the stock. I find that a little goes a long way.

Although the case consists of five parts of three different widths, they all begin at the same width. This makes it much easier to register the parts to each other when marking out dovetails and through-tenons. The door-frame parts also start out at the same thickness. Once the mortises and tenons are cut, it's easy to skim the front faces of the rails to create the insets. Finally, I use a hinge strip to mount the door, which allows me to easily inset the door from the front edge of the case. While the overall effect of all of these offsets is subtle, it would be difficult to create without having a solid game plan prior to construction. With some forethought, the process goes smoothly and accuracy is built into the workflow.

3

4

5

This cabinet offers another lesson in doing accurate work with a minimum of measuring. That might seem counterintuitive, but the more you rely on laying out joinery with marking gauges and spacer blocks instead of a ruler and pencil, the faster you'll work and the more fun you'll have. The actual dimensions of any project typically aren't that critical. Much more important is getting equal parts cut to equal lengths. Because of that, I tend to rely more on stop blocks when making cuts than I do on my tape measure.

Finally, while it might be tempting to mill all of the stock for the project at once, it's a better idea to start with the case parts and leave the door and drawer parts for later. This build-to-fit technique allows for changes along the way and takes the stress out of building to exact dimensions from the outset.

This build-to-fit technique allows for changes along the way and takes the stress out of building to exact dimensions from the outset.

DEALING WITH PROUD JOINERY

Making work with proud joinery can make things easier in that there's no need to flush parts after assembly. But that aspect poses a challenge as well, both in shaping the parts and avoiding glue squeeze-out. It helps to deal with both those issues prior to glue-up. I find it easier to chamfer the tenons and dovetails while the parts are still separate. To dial in the chamfer width, I'll block-plane a light chamfer on a shelf tenon, dry-fit the shelf, and check my progress. I like the chamfer to extend almost to the case side, but I definitely don't want it to extend into the joint. This would create a gap at the joint, so, if anything, I'll err on the side of a lighter chamfer. Once I have the width I want, I use that tenon as a visual guide for chamfering the rest of the shelf tenons as well as the pins and tails. It's tough to get a block plane between the tails, so I switch to a sanding block for those.

To deal with potential glue squeeze-out, I like to prefinish the parts with a washcoat of shellac (see p. 212). The shellac prevents any glue from adhering to the surface and protects the end grain. I use a 1-lb. cut and sand the parts after the shellac is dry. The shellac has the added benefit of raising and sealing the grain. Once it's sanded smooth, the final finish will flow on nicely and build quickly.

A SMOOTH SLIDING DRAWER

If you can cut a dovetail, you can make a dovetailed drawer. The process is fairly simple, but there are a few tricks to make sure that the drawer opens and closes smoothly without racking or scraping.

The most important task is to size the drawer front properly. The tighter the drawer fits side to side, the smoother it will slide. If a drawer sticks or racks when opening, it's probably too narrow for its opening. I get close at the tablesaw and then dial in the fit with a shooting board (**1**). If the case is slightly out of square, plane the ends of the drawer front to match. The drawer front should just be able to fit into the opening (**2**). The drawer height should have a little more wiggle room to allow for seasonal movement.

After cutting the joinery, I also like to take a few extra passes on the bottom edge to keep it from scraping on the case when opening and closing (**3**). When assembled, the side should extend below the front by $1/32$ in. or so (**4**).

VARIATIONS ON A THEME

Good design isn't just about a spark of inspiration—it's a constant conversation and rethinking as you build.

Sometimes it feels as though I make the same things over and over again. It's not so much a conscious decision as a compulsion of sorts. I make things that demand to be made, designs that demand to get out. I always work toward the same goal, in that I try to resist the temptation to make something more than it should be—fancy, impressive, important, or original—but instead make something that stays true to its nature as much as possible, as humble as that may be. However, nothing ever looks exactly the same even though my intent is always the same. While we build and transform raw materials into useful objects, we ourselves are transformed in the process. We change and grow, both in our skills and in our awareness.

In the same way that every dovetail we cut informs the next dovetail, so does every piece we make. Every struggle and frustration and failure and success moves us forward, so that while we may always strive for perfect, the definition of perfect that we hold in our minds is an ever-shifting target. Variation in our work is far more effective and substantive when we don't try so hard. "I made it like this, and then I decided to make it like this . . . ." Working from the logical side of the brain can lead to an endless collection of arrows surrounding the bullseye but never hitting the mark. That part of the brain is great for paying bills, getting to work on time, and flossing your teeth regularly, but it lacks the intuition needed to take the leaps of faith necessary to realize

An evolution of cabinets. "So how long did it take you to make that cabinet with the kumiko panel?" Well, on the one hand, about three days or so. On the other, about five years, because all of the other cabinets needed to happen before this one could be made.

an idea. Instead, listen for thoughts like, "I usually make it in oak, but I couldn't get ash out of my mind, but once I went with it, the dovetails didn't want to stick out as much and the drawer fronts wanted to be darker. I stayed with pine backboards but realized that I liked the way pine complemented the oak, but now it doesn't work with the ash and I think they need to come out, but I'm not sure where to go with it yet."

Good design isn't just about a spark of inspiration—it's a constant conversation and rethinking as you build. When you find yourself on that train, just let the project dictate where the destination needs to be. In that way, you may end up in a place you've never been, just by taking the same familiar route. It takes awareness, an open mind, and a clear-eyed view of the progress in spite of the effort that has already been invested. It takes a little fearlessness as well. When I first started out as an associate art director at *Fine Woodworking* magazine it would be scary to take an article layout in a different direction than I had originally envisioned. Bob Goodfellow, the magazine's art director at the time, would say that sometimes you just have to go down that path and see where it leads. Of course, then he'd smile and add, "Even if it's a dead end." Sometimes you just have to go there.

A CASE FOR KUMIKO

It was an idea that persisted, and a small cabinet without a home was a safe place to give it a try.

I teach a wall cabinet class fairly regularly, and I usually build the project along with the class. On one such cabinet, I wasn't happy with the way the frame-and-panel door turned out, so once I got it back to the shop, I decided to remake it. I used the occasion to try my hand at kumiko, a Japanese latticework technique most often associated with the *shoji* screens used in Japanese architecture. I had first seen it used in the furniture of John Reed Fox, a Massachusetts furniture maker, and had wanted to give it a try ever since.

In the new door I left an opening above the panel and filled it with a kumiko grid. The technique turned out to be easier than I expected, and I enjoyed the process as well. At first, I was worried that the delicate look might clash with the more rustic, heavy elements typical of my work. For me anyway, the kumiko turned out to be a nice counterpart to those elements, and it added some pop. But more than that, it felt like a natural step forward along the rather slow and winding design path I had been on. I was trying to avoid adding any arbitrary design details that would clutter and water down the work, but it was an idea that persisted, and a small cabinet without a home was a safe place to give it a try.

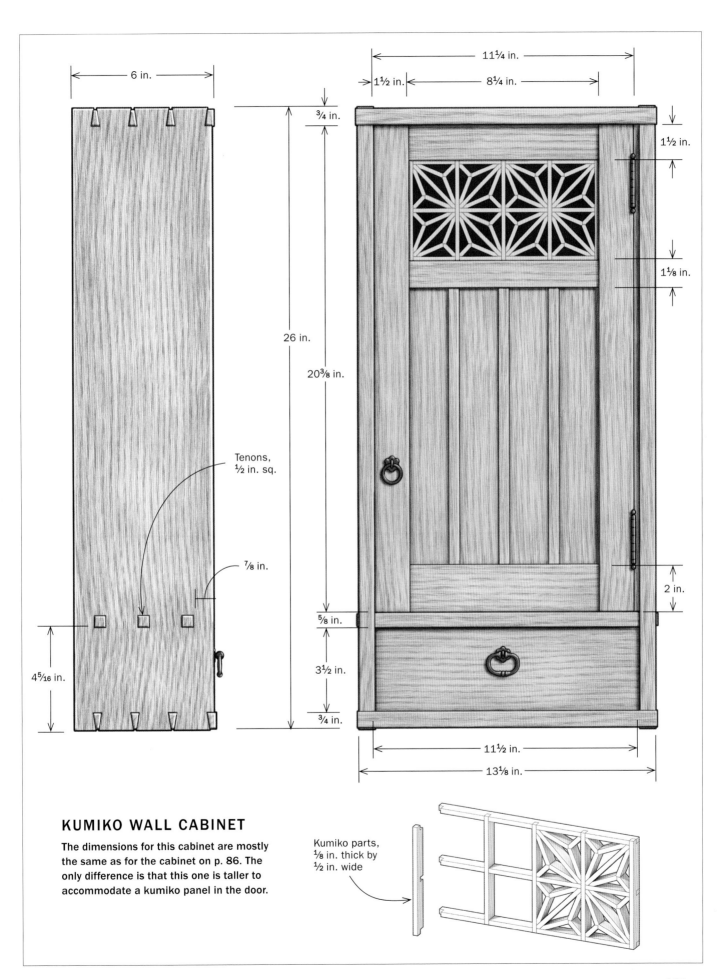

KUMIKO WALL CABINET

The dimensions for this cabinet are mostly the same as for the cabinet on p. 86. The only difference is that this one is taller to accommodate a kumiko panel in the door.

Tenons, ½ in. sq.

Kumiko parts, ⅛ in. thick by ½ in. wide

Making kumiko requires precise work, but I don't find it tedious or boring. I actually look forward to the quiet bench time the process affords, and the result is invariably a nice addition to a project.

I've used the technique in a number of pieces since then, from boxes to cabinets to case pieces, and my process has evolved over that time. I'd by no means call myself an expert on the technique, but the method I use is simple and yields good results for me (as well as for the many students I've taught it to). I make the kumiko stock at the tablesaw and handle the rest of the work with a sharp chisel and a pair of beveled guide blocks.

START WITH A SIMPLE DESIGN

While there are many different kumiko patterns, my work focuses on the *asa-no-ha*, or hemp leaf, pattern. It begins with notched strips that connect to form a square grid. Additional parts are then beveled to fit into the squares, creating the pattern. I make the bar grid using a finger-joint jig clamped to a tablesaw crosscut sled (see the sidebar "Start with a Grid"). The distance between the indexing pin on the jig and the sawblade determines the spacing of the grid. When sizing the panel to the door, I adjust the jig to create a grid that fits the frame snugly side to side. This spacing also determines the height of the grid and the resulting location of the center rail.

I typically use ¼-in.- or ½-in.-wide basswood or pine for the bars. Start by milling two pieces of stock to thickness. Then cut the notch for the half-lap joints in one blank

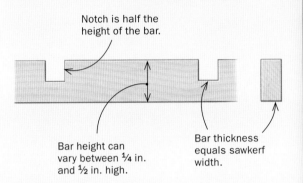

Notch is half the height of the bar.

Bar height can vary between ¼ in. and ½ in. high.

Bar thickness equals sawkerf width.

START WITH A GRID

The first step is to build the grid of half-lapped pieces, called bars. A simple finger-joint jig makes quick work of cutting the notches. To make the jig, cut a notch in a piece of MDF and glue in an indexing pin sized to match the notch. Then clamp the jig to a crosscut sled. The distance between the pin and the blade will determine the spacing of the grid (**1**).

Cut the notches in a wide piece of stock by cutting a dado, then placing it on the pin to cut the next dado (**2**). Rip the stock into individual bars (**3**). The thickness of the bars should match the notches. Use a thin-kerf blade to maximize yield and re-joint the stock as necessary to maintain a straight edge for ripping. To assemble the grid, cut the bars to length and add a dot of glue at each intersection. Work on a flat surface and make sure the bars are fully seated (**4**).

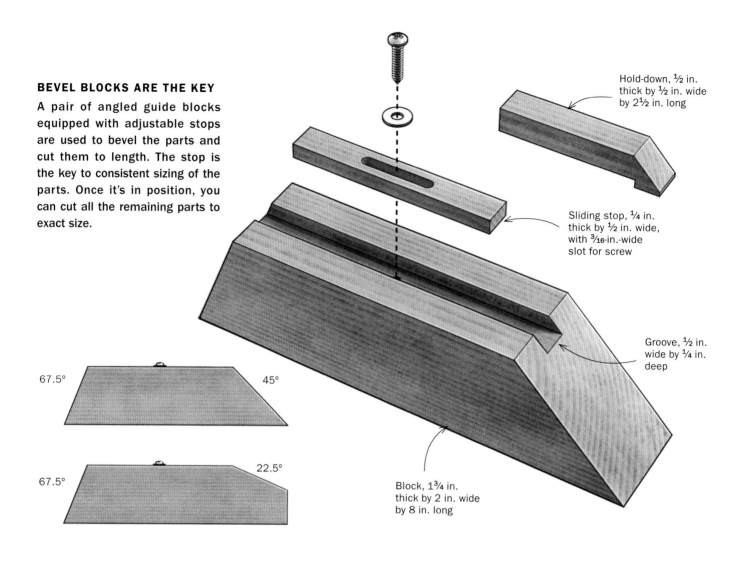

BEVEL BLOCKS ARE THE KEY
A pair of angled guide blocks equipped with adjustable stops are used to bevel the parts and cut them to length. The stop is the key to consistent sizing of the parts. Once it's in position, you can cut all the remaining parts to exact size.

Hold-down, ½ in. thick by ½ in. wide by 2½ in. long

Sliding stop, ¼ in. thick by ½ in. wide, with ³⁄₁₆-in.-wide slot for screw

Groove, ½ in. wide by ¼ in. deep

Block, 1¾ in. thick by 2 in. wide by 8 in. long

67.5°   45°

67.5°   22.5°

Although the design looks complex, it consists of only three uniquely sized parts. The key is repeatability when making them.

before ripping both into individual bars. The bars should fit snugly into the dadoes. I've planed the bars to final thickness in the past, but I find that using a sharp thin-kerf blade leaves a clean surface that doesn't require sanding or planing.

GUIDE BLOCKS MAKE FOR ACCURATE CHISEL WORK

Although the design looks complex, it consists of only three uniquely sized parts. The key is repeatability when making them. The ends of each part must be beveled at a specific angle, and the parts must be of consistent length. To tackle the job, I use a pair of beveled guide blocks with ends cut to various angles. A groove along the top holds the stock, and an adjustable stop sets the length of each part.

I start by making the long diagonal in each square using the 45° end of the bevel block. You'll need four pieces plus a couple more for test-fitting. Cut the pieces slightly overlong and set the stop block for a slightly longer piece than you think you need. Use a sharp chisel to make the first bevel, and then turn over the stock and finish the end, creating a centered point. Place the beveled end against the stop to bevel the opposite end. Check the fit in the grid, and adjust the stop as needed. You want a snug fit.

Next make the wings on either side of the diagonal. These parts are the most complex and numerous. You'll need a total of 16 to complete the design. Make at least

THE DIAGONALS FIRST

You need one diagonal per square, with both ends beveled at 45°. Make a few extra pieces to dial in the fit, which should be snug but not so tight that it forces the grid out of square. Sneak up on the fit. Set the sliding stop to cut the diagonal a little longer than needed (**1**). Place the stock against the stop and use a chisel to bevel one end (**2**). Flip the stock to create a center point. Rotate the stock and bevel the opposite end. Check the fit of the workpiece (**3**).

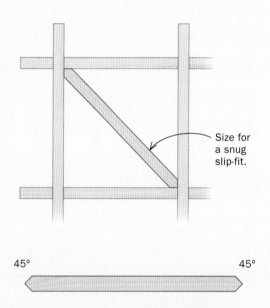

Size for a snug slip-fit.

45°   45°

ADD THE WINGS

The ends of the wings get multiple angles. Use a pair of guide blocks with slightly different stop settings to cut the 67.5° off-center bevel on all of the parts (**1**). Then cut a 22.5° bevel on the opposite ends (**2**). Adjust the stop so that the parts fully seat in the corners when the wings are butted together (**3**).

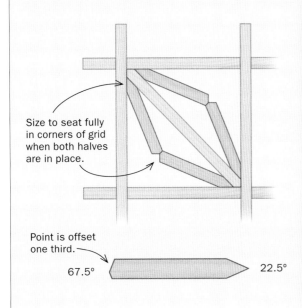

Size to seat fully in corners of grid when both halves are in place.

Point is offset one third.

67.5° 22.5°

four extra parts for test-fitting. The wings have a centered 22.5° bevel on the outer end and an off-center 67.5° bevel where the parts meet. I start with the off-center bevel, using the 67.5° end of each guide block. Again, start with parts that are slightly oversize. Set one stop block to cut a bevel on one end. Then set the stop on the second block to cut a shorter bevel, creating a point that is roughly one-third the width of the stock.

Bevel one end of all the pieces this way before using the 22.5° block to bevel the opposite end. To determine the correct length, make two pieces and fit them in place so their ends meet. Then look at how the outside ends are seated. They should fit snugly in the corner of the square. If there's a gap at the bottom of the joint, the pieces are too long. A gap at the top means they're too short.

Complete the design with short diagonals that lock the wings in place. You can leave the parts dry-fitted, but for parts that see a lot of action like doors and box tops, I glue them in place. To do this, I slip the parts out one square at a time, maintaining their orientation. Then I reassemble them in the same order, using a sharpened stick to place a drop of glue at each intersection as I go. Once the glue is dry, trim off the tabs and level the assembly by rubbing it on a piece of 220-grit sandpaper on a flat surface. I leave the kumiko unfinished.

KEYSTONES LOCK IT IN PLACE

You'll need two short diagonal pieces per square. Each end is beveled at 45°; size for a snug fit. The keystones secure all the pieces in the square.

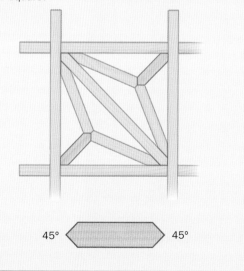

45°   45°

SOMETHING AT THE WAISTLINE

There are many things I am not—a finisher, a carver, a turner, a mechanic, or a carpenter, to name but a few—but woodworking requires that we wear all of those hats now and again. When it comes to chip carving, I'm far from an expert. OK, there's your fair warning. Now let me tell you how I go about carving a really simple little detail that adds a little interest to a piece.

One place I like to use chip carving is on the edge of a shelf on a wall cabinet. It turns an otherwise-overlooked element in the cabinet into the star of the show. The diamond pattern is created by carving opposing triangles along the stock, leaving just the diamonds remaining. The process involves a pair of angled chops, followed by a shallow cut to pop out the waste. The key is accurate layout: If you're not right on, everything starts to look a little wonky.

I use a combination square to draw out the pattern along the stock; the only trick is to make sure the pattern is centered along the length. It's rare that the pattern terminates exactly at the ends, so I usually stop it short and leave a space at each end. As long as it's centered, it looks as though you planned it that way.

The carving goes quickly and requires just a single tool. Try it out on a sample board and you'll get the hang of it before too long. After a while, you'll find a rhythm to your cuts that will yield a consistent pattern.

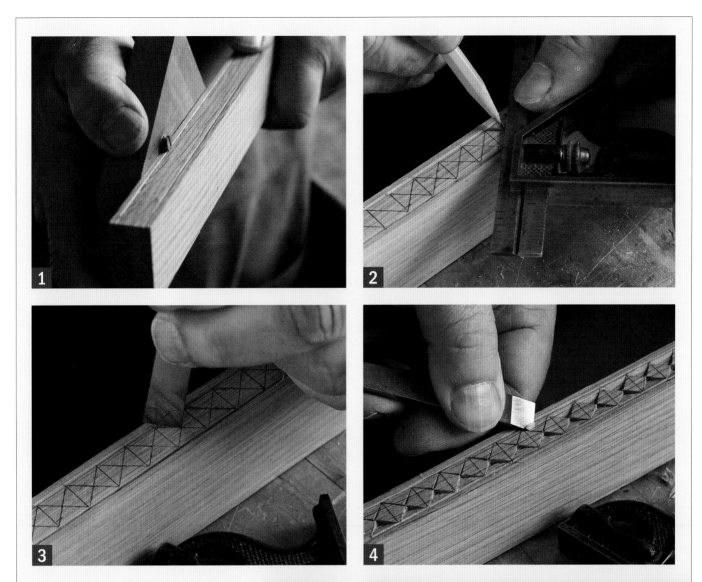

A SIMPLE CHIP CARVING

A flat-head screw makes a good scratch stock to establish the bead on each edge of the pattern (**1**). Lay out the pattern starting at the center and work toward each end (**2**). Then grab a sharp chisel and make angled cuts along the diagonals, starting where they intersect (**3**). Tilt the chisel so that you make a cut about $\frac{1}{16}$ in. deep at the center and angling to zero at the outside corner. Make a shallow angled cut to remove the triangle of waste (**4**). The key is consistency, both in the angle of the chisel and the force of the strike. Round the corners to complete the bead once you're finished (**5**).

AN INCOMPLETE CABINET

When I started out woodworking, an idea that I accepted without question was that the point of making was to make something. Pretty obvious, right? Focus on the object, and once you get it to where you want it to go, you're done, it's done, finished. Unfortunately, it didn't always feel that way. The piece might be finished, but somehow it still felt incomplete—not incomplete in the sense that there's something else left to do, but incomplete in that it's somehow missing something. When we build objects that we intend to put to use, we leave voids—an empty drawer or box, a bare shelf or tabletop—and in those voids and bare surfaces lies the incompleteness of what we make. It's not until our work gets put to use, when the objects intended to be stored, protected, or displayed are added to the mix, that the equation is finally complete. That's when the work has the chance to come alive and take on its true nature.

There is another notion of "incompleteness" that I'm beginning to realize the importance of as well. Its genesis goes back to Wall Cabinet no. 1 (right). While that cabinet is nice enough on its own, what really brought it to life for me was a little teapot that I decided to place on the center shelf when photographing it. There was a quiet hum to it that neither the cabinet nor the teapot alone could quite conjure, but together the two separate notes joined into a resonant chord. It opened my eyes to the notion that an object's contents could enhance the beauty of the object itself.

A cabinet with shelves and a drawer or two, and maybe a small door, invites interaction while still adding to the melody.

I began to see that while a plain wall shelf quickly disappears into the background when filled, and a cabinet completely enclosed with a door allows for no interaction with its contents at all, a cabinet with open shelves and a drawer or two, and maybe a small door, invites interaction while still adding to the melody.

This cabinet falls into that category. There are drawers and a door that allow me to show off just a bit, but also plenty of open shelf space that lets the contents be the star of the show as well. It was built to house an ever-growing collection of pottery, and the more the shelves fill up the more I like the cabinet.

While I've built similar cabinets out of oak alone, this one has a case made of ash. I usually look for lighter ash boards, especially when I pair ash with oak. But I'd found a pair of boards that had a dark, even tone to them and decided to put them to use on the cabinet. I had planned on white oak for the drawer fronts but was worried that there wouldn't be enough contrast with the darker ash, so I used brown oak instead. Brown oak is a fantastic wood with a chocolate brown color and a slightly finer grain than white oak. Unfortunately, it's expensive and hard to come by where I live. I have

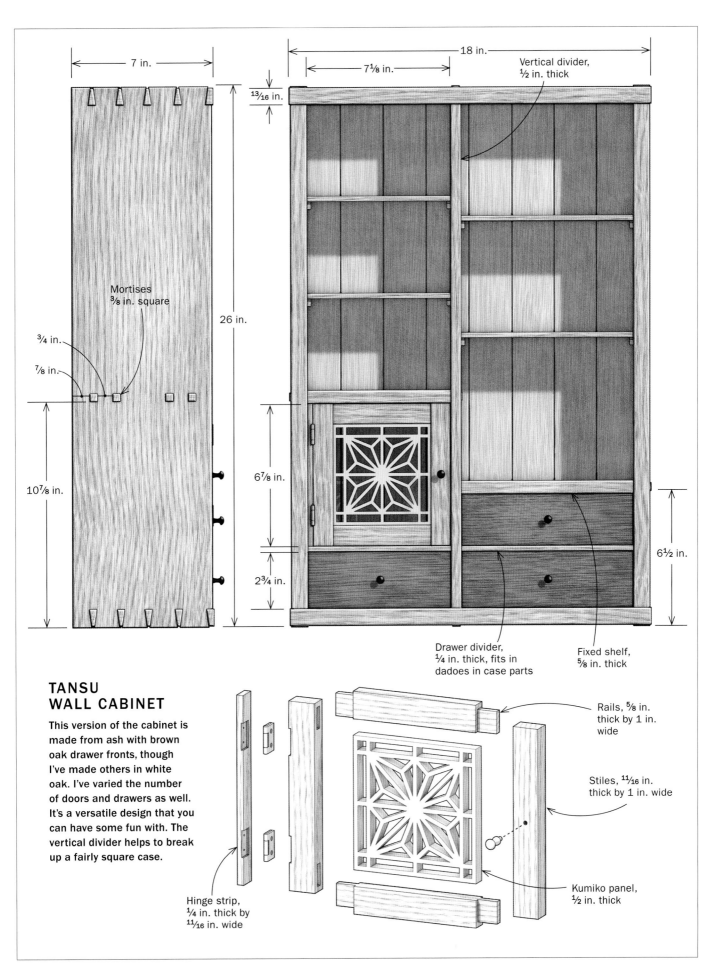

7 in.

13/16 in.

18 in.

7 1/8 in.

Vertical divider,
1/2 in. thick

Mortises
3/8 in. square

3/4 in.

7/8 in.

26 in.

10 7/8 in.

6 7/8 in.

2 3/4 in.

6 1/2 in.

Drawer divider,
1/4 in. thick, fits in
dadoes in case parts

Fixed shelf,
5/8 in. thick

TANSU WALL CABINET

This version of the cabinet is made from ash with brown oak drawer fronts, though I've made others in white oak. I've varied the number of doors and drawers as well. It's a versatile design that you can have some fun with. The vertical divider helps to break up a fairly square case.

Rails, 5/8 in. thick by 1 in. wide

Stiles, 11/16 in. thick by 1 in. wide

Kumiko panel, 1/2 in. thick

Hinge strip, 1/4 in. thick by 11/16 in. wide

a small stash that I save for special occasions, and I'm happy that I parted with some of it for this project. The door presented a convenient opportunity to include a square of kumiko latticework.

AVOIDING A CLUNKY LOOK

All of the vertical and horizontal dividers and shelves add up to a lot of elements on the face of the cabinet. To create a sense of structure and lighten the look as much as possible, it's important to graduate the thickness of the parts.

A general rule of thumb that I follow is to start with thicker stock on the outside of a cabinet to help frame it, and then get gradually thinner with interior parts to avoid looking too heavy. A lesson I learned from Garrett Hack, a Vermont furniture maker who builds delicate-looking but sturdy furniture, is that you can go a lot thinner with parts than you might expect and still get the necessary strength from them. A wall cabinet shelf with a short span, for instance, can be as thin as ¼ in. without the risk of sagging.

While it takes a little more work to mill stock in a variety of thicknesses and account for them when cutting joinery, the result is worth it compared to a cabinet made completely from, say, ¾-in. stock. This cabinet offers a good lesson in that strategy, but just about every piece I make uses it to a certain extent. Take a look at the dimensioned drawings throughout the book and you'll begin to spot it. It's a subtle thing, but the simpler the work is, the more important details like this are.

You can go a lot thinner with parts than you might expect and still get the necessary strength from them.

CHAPTER 5

BOXES & CHESTS

Whenever I ask a new woodworker what they've been building, the answer is invariably, "Oh, nothing much, a few boxes and such. I don't really have the machines or a shop set up to make bigger stuff." Boxes do seem to be the most common way to jump into the craft, but the notion that they're easier to make because they're small is just not true. First, we tend to come in closest contact with a box: We pick it up, we open the lid. We look at it up close, so any inaccuracies are more apparent on a box than on a large piece of furniture. Second, the scale of a box is small so that any minor gap is relatively large compared to its overall size. Also, wood choice is incredibly important, and if you're trying to make do with scraps, it's a tough way to start.

So if you're giving yourself a hard time because you "can't even get a box right," you're not alone and you're probably getting along better than it might seem. That's not to say that boxes aren't fun to make. They do offer a lot of woodworking in a small package and you can get through them fairly quickly, so your learning curve regarding both craftsmanship and design can progress at a good rate. When you step up to chests and start to add doors and drawers, your woodworking journey really takes off.

A QUICK-TO-MAKE BOX IS NOT A BAD THING

*Trying to make any-
thing of quality out
of wood that can be
sold at a relatively
low price is a really
hard thing to do.*

I've probably made more mitered boxes than all the other pieces I've made combined. One year, my wife, Rachel, was sewing some napkins and aprons to sell
at holiday craft fairs. She asked if I could come up with a wood "something" to
sell along with them. Trying to make anything of quality out of wood that can be sold
at a relatively low price is a really hard thing to do. Dovetails were definitely out of
the question, but a cutting board glued up from strips of wood or a mitered box that
I could make with tablesaw joinery might get me in the ballpark. But just because it
was something that I could set up to produce in quantity didn't necessarily mean that
I could knock it out without any thought. The exercise was actually a good learning
experience, and it offered a valuable insight into making clean, precise work. In the
end, I made two styles of boxes: a small box with a rabbeted lid for salt, and a larger
box with a sawn-off lid for tea packets.

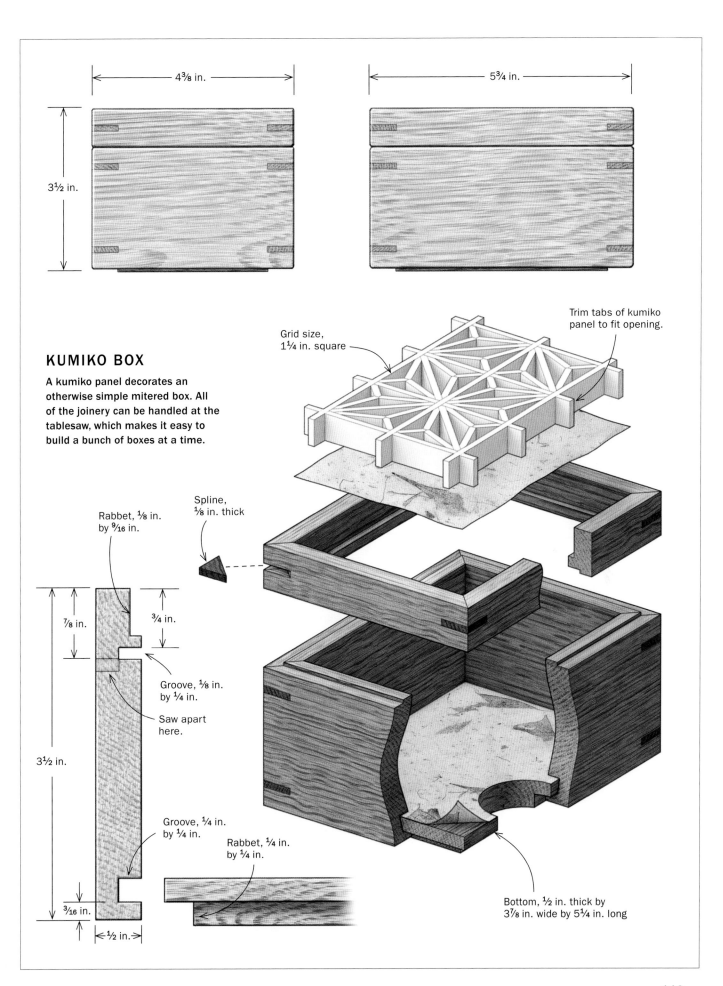

4³⁄₈ in.

5³⁄₄ in.

3¹⁄₂ in.

KUMIKO BOX

A kumiko panel decorates an otherwise simple mitered box. All of the joinery can be handled at the tablesaw, which makes it easy to build a bunch of boxes at a time.

Grid size, 1¹⁄₄ in. square

Trim tabs of kumiko panel to fit opening.

Rabbet, ¹⁄₈ in. by ⁹⁄₁₆ in.

Spline, ¹⁄₈ in. thick

⁷⁄₈ in.

³⁄₄ in.

Groove, ¹⁄₈ in. by ¹⁄₄ in.

Saw apart here.

3¹⁄₂ in.

Groove, ¹⁄₄ in. by ¹⁄₄ in.

Rabbet, ¹⁄₄ in. by ¹⁄₄ in.

Bottom, ¹⁄₂ in. thick by 3⁷⁄₈ in. wide by 5¹⁄₄ in. long

³⁄₁₆ in.

¹⁄₂ in.

While my initial focus was on cranking out something fast to sell cheaply, I realized that making the boxes provided an opportunity to reach people who admire hand-made work but couldn't otherwise afford a larger piece. With that understanding, I made sure that I didn't put in any less of an effort to do my best work on the boxes than I would on bigger projects. That said, when faced with a run of 20 or 30 boxes at a time, my focus was definitely on efficiency. I milled extra stock, and if there were any defects in a part, it went in the scrap pile without hesitation. I also focused on an economy of actions, because a savings of a few seconds per part at each stage of the process added up to a significant impact on my earnings per hour.

If I had thought about it beforehand, I would have said that such a focus would result in a consistent though not necessarily high quality of workmanship. The opposite actually turned out to be the case. Because of the repetition and the willingness to throw out anything less than perfect, the little boxes that I thought I was just banging out were incredibly clean and precise and had the level of workmanship that I would wish on all of my work. One warning though: Once you start to make boxes like these

GROOVES, THEN MITERS

The great thing about making a mitered box is that you can run grooves and rabbets and such while the parts are still long. For this box, there's a groove for the bottom, a rabbet for the kumiko panel, and a second groove that will create a lip once the lid is cut off (**1**). I use a simple jig that screws to my miter gauge to cut the miters. It has a hold-down and a pair of hinged stops that allow me to cut all four sides of the box without having to reposition the stops. Every time I use the jig, I slide it over just a little so that the blade cuts a fresh edge. Start by mitering one end of the stock (**2**). Then position the mitered end against a stop and miter the opposite end (**3**).

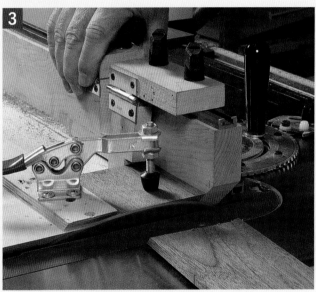

MITER JIG

This simple-to-make sled screws to your miter gauge. The aluminum T-track and hardware are available from Rockler.com (part number 24063).

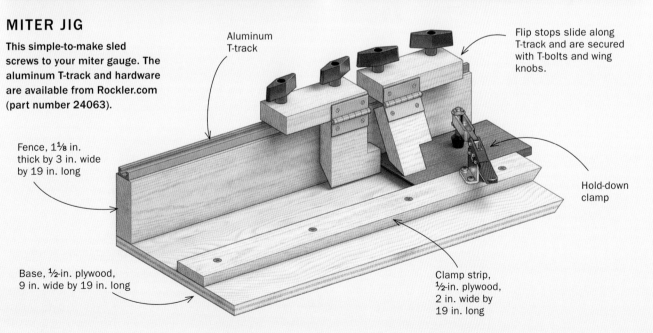

Aluminum T-track

Flip stops slide along T-track and are secured with T-bolts and wing knobs.

Fence, 1⅛ in. thick by 3 in. wide by 19 in. long

Hold-down clamp

Base, ½-in. plywood, 9 in. wide by 19 in. long

Clamp strip, ½-in. plywood, 2 in. wide by 19 in. long

GLUE AND SPLINE THE BOX

I like to line the bottom of the box with handmade paper. You can find a variety of colors at most art supply stores. It's easiest to spray the box bottom with a light mist of adhesive, drop it onto the paper, and trim around it (**1**). The next step is to glue up the box with the bottom in place. Wipe a thin coat of shellac on the inside faces to prevent glue squeeze-out from sticking. Arrange the sides in order on the bench and stretch tape across them. Flip them over and roll everything up with the bottom in place to make sure it fits (**2**). Unroll the sides and glue the miters for final assembly. Be sure to pull the tape tight to avoid gaps at the last corner (**3**).

Once the glue is dry, I use a jig that supports the box at 45° to cut slots for splines at the tablesaw (**4**). The blade height will determine the length of the slots on the box sides. Be sure not to cut through to the inside of the box when cutting the slots. Then glue splines into the slots (**5**). When the glue is dry, I use a stationary belt sander to sand everything flush.

1

Even if you're making only a box or two, it pays to mill up a bunch of stock for the box sides. Once you have, you can knock out a box at another time pretty quickly.

and sell them, you will have unending requests to make more. Every friend and family member that owns a box and is looking for a special gift or house-warming present will give you a call. Don't even get me started on cutting boards . . . .

The notion that because boxes are small they're a good way to use up scraps falls flat when you're faced with making them in quantity. Stock prep is incredibly important for the rest of the process to go smoothly. Even if you're making only a box or two, it pays to mill up a bunch of stock for the box sides. Once you have, you can knock out a box at another time pretty quickly. Remember those last-minute gift requests?

The good thing about a mitered box is that all of the machining can be done prior to cutting the miters, so the work goes fast. To cut the miters, I made a simple sled for the tablesaw equipped with a pair of hinged stop blocks (see "Grooves, then Miters," p. 121). This allowed me to cut the sides and ends in sequence—long, short, long, short—so that the grain continued uninterrupted from side to side. Dialing in the miter is crucial, and the best way to do it is to miter four pieces, run a strip of tape across the backs, and wrap them together to see if the final joint closes. Take your time to get it right before cutting into your good stock.

The style of box I make and teach now has a kumiko panel that drops into a rabbet along the top edge of the box. It also has a built-in lip so the top and bottom register to one another when closed. I create the lip by cutting a groove halfway through the stock on the inside face before mitering and glue-up. When sawing off the lid, I again set the blade to cut halfway and adjust the fence so the groove on the outside is offset lower than the groove on the inside face. Once the lid is sawn off, the lips are created automatically.

Before cutting off the lid, however, I cut slots on the corners of the box for splines. The splines reinforce the miter joints and add a little interest to the box. I use a simple jig that holds the box at 45° to cut the slots at the tablesaw. A flat-top blade leaves a square bottom for the spline to fit into.

The bottom of the box is rabbeted to fit into a groove in the sides. A nice touch is to line the bottom with handmade paper before gluing it in place. I also place paper into the rabbet in the lid before dropping the kumiko panel in place.

SAW OFF THE LID AND ADD THE PANEL

To saw off the lid, set the blade to half the thickness of the stock and offset it a blade's width down from the slot on the inside of the box. Save an offcut to help with setup. Start with the ends when cutting, making sure to keep the box against the fence (**1**). The joint will need a little cleanup, but the saw will give you a good head start (**2**). I like to drop paper onto the rabbet before installing the panel (**3**). Trim the ends of the kumiko panel to fit the rabbet (**4**). I like a snug fit, but if it's a little loose, a drop of glue at each tab will hold it in place.

A TEA BOX WITH OYSTERS AND PEARLS IN MIND

The outside, the inside, its contents, and the reaction of the user: Boxes provide a fun handful of puzzle pieces to play with.

I always think of boxes in terms of what they will hold—and how they'll be held and who will hold them. If I don't, they tend to stay empty or get filled with a random assortment of spare change, movie ticket stubs, and golf tees. When thinking about the contents, the notion of protection comes to mind as well: protection from the elements, or from damage during travel, or maybe just a separation from other aspects of life in general. A box also offers the opportunity for surprise. As inspiration for this box, I'd been thinking about oysters, and how their rough, rocklike shells with their iridescent interior protect their delicate contents (and maybe even a pearl waiting inside). Protection, surprise, a roughness hiding a treasure inside—somehow the picture was coming into focus. The outside, the inside, its contents, and the reaction of the user: Boxes provide a fun handful of puzzle pieces to play with.

Like just about everything I make, this tea box had a long gestation in the belly of many boxes and projects that came before it. I had made a few boxes featuring proud dovetails and mitered liners, but a design flaw in a particular box presented the opportunity for a new element in the guise of a fix. Rather than just a shallow lip of the liner providing registration for the lid, I had the idea to extend it above the sides for a fun visual surprise as well.

It wasn't a big deal to accomplish this. I just sawed off the lid lower, so that as the box was opened, more of the liner was exposed. The design flaw was that the deep lid made it difficult to pick up the box with one hand without accidentally grabbing just the lid by mistake. I didn't like the idea of a two-handed box, so I needed to figure out a way to keep the lid in place while it was carried but for it to be easily removable once it reached its destination. Some sort of twine or cord came

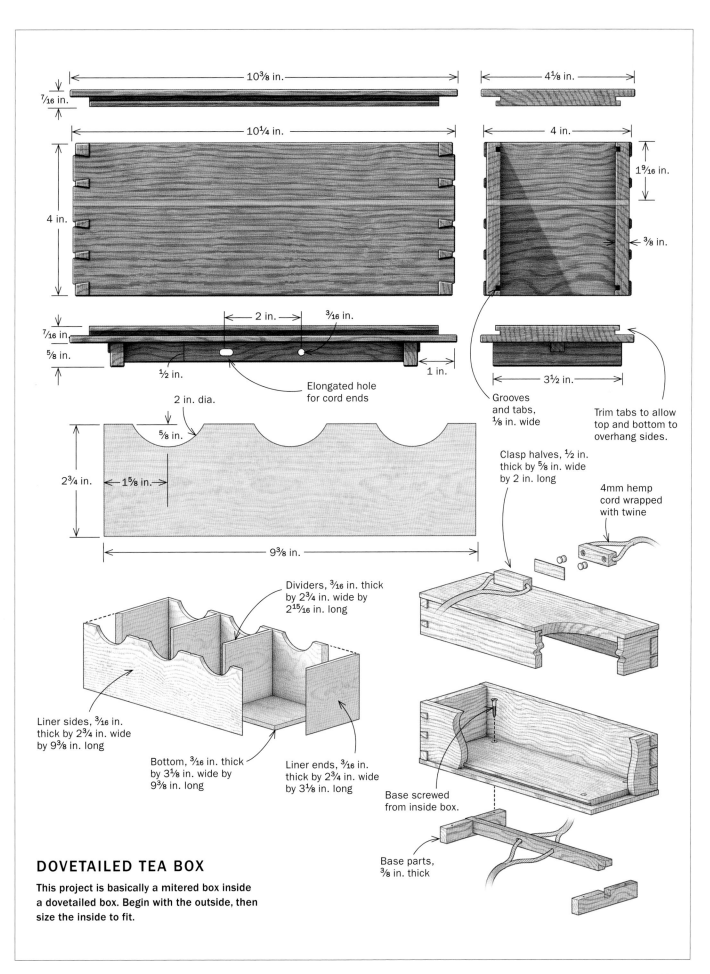

10⅜ in.

7/16 in.

4⅛ in.

10¼ in.

4 in.

4 in.

1⁹/₁₆ in.

⅜ in.

7/16 in.

⅝ in.

2 in.

3/16 in.

½ in.

Elongated hole for cord ends

1 in.

3½ in.

Grooves and tabs, ⅛ in. wide

Trim tabs to allow top and bottom to overhang sides.

2 in. dia.

⅝ in.

2¾ in.

1⅝ in.

9⅜ in.

Clasp halves, ½ in. thick by ⅝ in. wide by 2 in. long

4mm hemp cord wrapped with twine

Dividers, 3/16 in. thick by 2¾ in. wide by 2¹⁵/₁₆ in. long

Liner sides, 3/16 in. thick by 2¾ in. wide by 9⅜ in. long

Bottom, 3/16 in. thick by 3⅛ in. wide by 9⅜ in. long

Liner ends, 3/16 in. thick by 2¾ in. wide by 3⅛ in. long

Base screwed from inside box.

Base parts, ⅜ in. thick

DOVETAILED TEA BOX

This project is basically a mitered box inside a dovetailed box. Begin with the outside, then size the inside to fit.

BUILDING WITH A LIGHT LOOK

Boxes have a tendency to look clunky if you're not careful. A general rule I follow is to start with stock as thin as possible. When that isn't enough, the next step is to make the components look thin even when they're not. The top and bottom of this box are a good example. The box parts are ⅜ in. thick, which was as thin as I could go and still groove the sides without making them too weak. I wanted the look of a thin overhanging top, but that would have been difficult to attach and may have warped over time. The solution was to groove the sides and the top (**1**) so they could lock together, leaving a thin tab overhanging the sides (**2**). Not only did this make the top look thinner, but it also concealed the thickness of the sides.

To open up the grain and add some texture to the wenge, hit it with a wire brush and wipe on a coat of shellac before gluing up the box (**3**). Glue up the box with the top and bottom in place (**4**). Then slice the lid off of the box at the bandsaw (**5**).

I'd built similar boxes in a variety of woods, but everything seemed to come together when I decided to use up some scraps of wenge I had lying around.

to mind, but not just a knot to tie it at the top. Maybe a bead and loop? That sounded a little clunky.

The clasp of my wife's vintage handbag sparked the idea of a clasp to hold the halves of the cord together. On my early efforts I made a clasp with a sliding dovetail. It's an elegant solution, but the precise machining involved in making it wasn't exactly the way I wanted to be spending my time in the shop. So a simpler solution that relies on embedded magnets has become my clasp of choice. I also added a base to the box in order to provide clearance for the cord to wrap underneath as well as a means to secure the ends. The cord is threaded through the clasp halves and through a pair of holes in the base. Once I had the clasp centered and the right amount of tension, I drove a wedged dowel into the hole in the base where the ends of the cord threaded though to lock everything in place.

I'd built similar boxes in a variety of woods, but everything seemed to come together when I decided to use up some scraps of wenge I had lying around. (And it was on this box that I first resorted to taping the ends of the boards before scribing the dovetails in order to see the knife lines.) Although I liked the look of the wenge, a dark, hard wood, it was a little plain and tended to show fingerprints. On a whim, I pulled out a wire brush and gave the box a good scrub. A wonderful texture emerged along with a hard polish, which brought the oyster shell to mind once again.

For the liner, I put a board of tight tiger maple to good use, mimicking the mother of pearl inside a shell. Since then, I've used bird's-eye and spalted maple to good

A mitered liner finishes out the interior and offers a nice surprise when you lift off the lid. The parts are first fit to the box and then removed and glued together as a single unit. (See p. 136 to learn how to make mitered dividers.)

The bandsaw marks of the clasp, the open grain of the wenge, and the rough hemp cord all joined together in a way that opened my eyes to the possibilities that texture can provide.

effect as well. I made the clasp from ebony, but its cold shark-eye black surface seemed out of place. I held my breath (and would have crossed my fingers had they not been needed) and slid the clasp across a bandsaw blade taking a light skim cut to texture the surface. A little steel wool and wax gave it a hard shine as well. Suddenly, the box became a really interesting symphony of textures. The bandsaw marks of the clasp, the open grain of the wenge, and the rough hemp cord all joined together in a way that opened my eyes to the possibilities that texture can provide.

On my first attempt at adding the cord and clasp, the two strands of cord paralleled each other on the sides of the box, and I was bothered that the pair tended not to stay aligned. When I brought the box into the office to show it off just a little, my boss at the time looked at it and said, "Yeah, I know what you're going for, but I don't think you're there yet." I wanted to argue, but I knew he was right.

As I looked at it, I thought why not bind the pair of cords together on the sides? The thinner twine I used to bind the cords created yet another texture in a smaller scale, which seemed to tie into the size of the box better than the thicker cord alone. Binding the cords also revealed an unexpected pair of triangles across the top as the cords angled from the clasp toward each other. At first I took a guess as to where to start and stop the wrap. Now I add a pair of twist ties to each side and use them as a guide when starting and stopping the wrap. The pair of cords tend to twist a little when wrapping them, so I make it a habit to straighten them out periodically as I go.

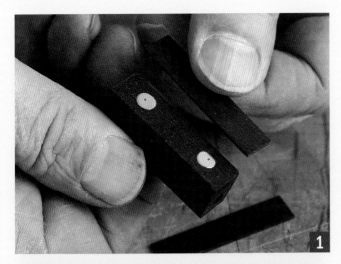

A HEMP AND EBONY CLASP

The clasp itself is simple to make. Drill the ebony stock for the hemp cord and magnets. Drop a pair of ¼-in. magnets into each hole and cap the face with a thin strip of ebony (**1**). Thread the cord through the clasp and the box base. Add twist ties at the top and bottom of the box sides to mark the start and stop of the twine wrap (**2**). Once everything is in place and there isn't any slack in the cord, drive a wedge through the holes in the base to secure the cord ends (**3**). Wrap the cord with thinner twine for a clean look (**4 & 5**). See the sewing table on p. 189 to learn how to secure the twine at each end of the wrap.

FLY ME TO THE MOON

As the door was slid from one side of the case to the other, more and more dark walnut drawers were exposed and the overall effect was that of the changing phases of the Moon. So it became the Moon jewelry chest.

I hate to waste a good dovetail, and, when demonstrating, I tend to cut a bunch of them. It doesn't matter how many dovetails you've seen, you never tire of seeing just one more. I'm the same way. Rather than come home with a pile of sample joints, I try to mill up a few boards so that I at least return with a dovetailed rectangle that could find its way into a box or chest of some sort. I like having the dovetailed boards around my shop. They tend to find a spot and gather dust, but they're always in the corner of my vision as well. They must get into my mind somehow, because eventually I'll know just what to do with them.

One such rectangle became the Moon jewelry chest. It was a long shape that presented an opportunity to try my hand at a sliding door, something I'd wanted to make for a while. It wasn't deep enough to handle a pair of doors nested one behind the other, so I made just a single half-width door. I wanted there to be an open and closed position, so the solution I came up with was to make half of the drawers in white oak, which the case was made of as well. The other half was made from walnut. The idea was that with the oak drawers exposed the door was in the closed position, because the case, door, and drawers all matched. When the door was slid to reveal the walnut drawers, they represented the inside of the case.

In the end, it seemed to work well enough, but I was left with a few challenges. First, the door was wider than it was high, which gave it a clunky look. To solve that problem, I divided the door panel with a number of vertical slats. These slats created a strong vertical element, which counteracted the horizontal shape of the door. The second challenge was to figure a way to get a handle on the drawers. Literally. They sat right behind the sliding door and there wasn't enough room for a normal pull. I had considered drilling a hole in each front that a finger could fit inside of, but that seemed too crude. I ended up taking a halfway approach, carving a shallow recess and mounting a pull in the center. This kept the pull from sticking out too far, but still allowed you to get a grip on it. When finished, it looked like a series of lunar craters across the face of the chest. As the door was slid from one side of the case to the other, more and more dark walnut drawers were exposed and the overall effect was that of the changing phases of the Moon. So it became the Moon jewelry chest.

I wouldn't call it an accident as much as an exercise in solving a series of problems. While a dovetailed case was familiar enough, this project introduced some new elements that have found their way into subsequent pieces. I've used vertical slats to

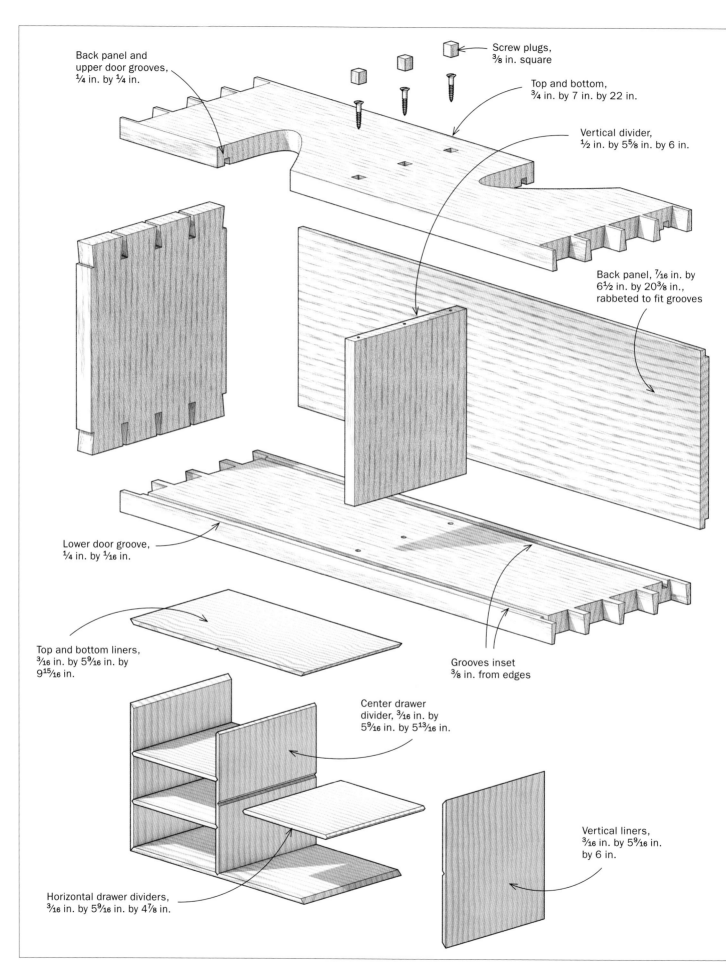

Back panel and upper door grooves, ¼ in. by ¼ in.

Screw plugs, ⅜ in. square

Top and bottom, ¾ in. by 7 in. by 22 in.

Vertical divider, ½ in. by 5⅝ in. by 6 in.

Back panel, ⁷⁄₁₆ in. by 6½ in. by 20⅜ in., rabbeted to fit grooves

Lower door groove, ¼ in. by ¹⁄₁₆ in.

Top and bottom liners, ³⁄₁₆ in. by 5⁹⁄₁₆ in. by 9¹⁵⁄₁₆ in.

Grooves inset ⅜ in. from edges

Center drawer divider, ³⁄₁₆ in. by 5⁹⁄₁₆ in. by 5¹³⁄₁₆ in.

Vertical liners, ³⁄₁₆ in. by 5⁹⁄₁₆ in. by 6 in.

Horizontal drawer dividers, ³⁄₁₆ in. by 5⁹⁄₁₆ in. by 4⅞ in.

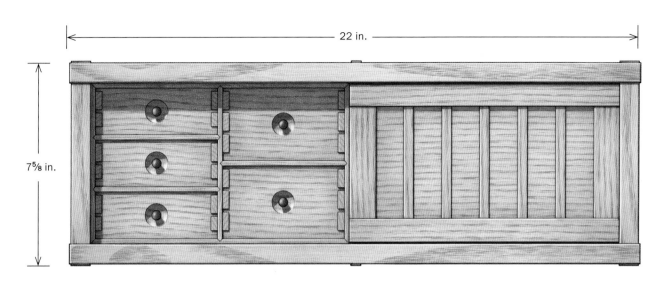

MOON JEWELRY CHEST

Although final lengths are given for the door parts and dividers, wait until the case is built before cutting them to final length. To prevent the long case from possibly bowing, the center divider is screwed in place.

Door rail, ½ in. by 1 in. by 10⁷⁄₁₆ in.

Door stile, ½ in. by 1 in. by 6³⁄₁₆ in.; trim ¹⁄₁₆ in. off front face after cutting joinery.

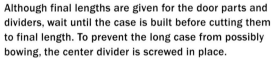

Sides, ¾ in. by 7 in. by 7⁵⁄₈ in.

Door panel, ¼ in. by 4⁹⁄₁₆ in. by 8¹³⁄₁₆ in.

Mullions, ⅛ in. by ⅜ in., inset into ¹⁄₁₆-in.-deep dadoes after door glue-up

Recess for pull, ¼ in. deep by ¾ in. dia.

Drawer front, ⅜ in. thick

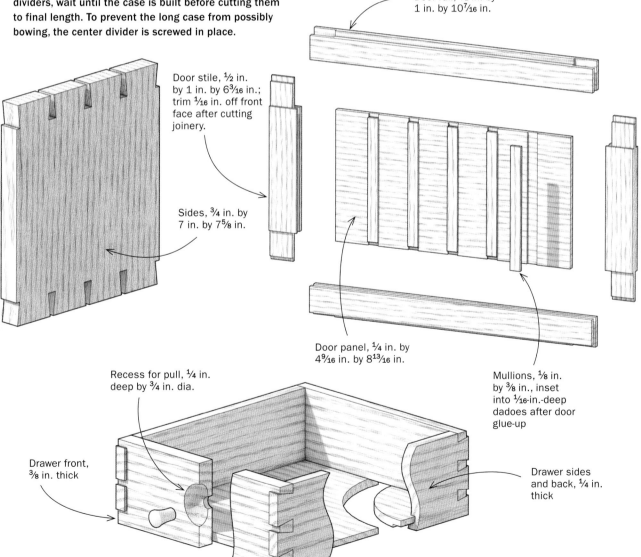

Drawer sides and back, ¼ in. thick

ADDING A MITERED LINING

The mitered lining is supported by the outer case, so you can make it from thin stock and still have plenty of strength. I usually aim for a ³⁄₁₆-in. thickness. The corners are joined with miters and the dividers are beveled to fit into V-grooves.

One way to tackle all of the joints is with a V-groove bit at the router table. Start by cutting the stock to length with square ends. The outer pieces should fit the case snugly end to end. To size the dividers, add one of the outer pieces against the case and fit the divider between it and the opposite case side. This will account for the bevels that fit halfway into each outer piece.

To miter the outer pieces, set the bit higher than the stock and bury it in the fence so that it cuts a miter without reducing the length of the piece (**1**). To bevel the ends of the dividers, lower the bit so that it cuts a miter half the thickness of the stock. Make a pass and then flip the stock to complete the bevel. For the V-grooves, set the height of the bit to half the thickness of the stock. Use a push pad to keep the stock against the table for a consistent-depth groove (**2**). There's a good chance the pieces won't quite fit once you try to install them all together in the case. I use a shooting board that supports my plane at 45° to fine-tune the fit (**3**).

Continue trimming the parts until they all fit snugly into the case, beginning with the outer pieces and finishing with the dividers (**4**). Once everything is cut to size, remove the parts and glue them together, using tape as a clamp as you would a mitered box (**5**). Sometimes additional light clamping pressure is needed over the dividers to make sure there are no gaps. Finally, install each section of dividers (**6**), inserting the center divider in between.

An idea I borrowed from the traditional spice boxes was an assembly of mitered dividers to house the drawers.

divide a panel many times. A sliding door and recessed pulls have made their way into a number of pieces as well. While working toward an individual style can be described in terms of assembling a set of design elements that create a consistent style between projects, I tend to think in terms of assembling an arsenal of problem solvers. A lot of my design efforts aren't devoted to making something look unique as much as getting rid of as many things that bug me as possible. One thing that can't be overstated is that I was able to try out all of these solutions in a risk-free setting. It was just a rectangle left over from a dovetail demo gathering dust in the corner of my shop. There wasn't a client or class or reader to worry about. There wasn't a huge investment in materials. It was a safe place to make a mistake, a safe place to play.

An idea I borrowed from the traditional spice boxes was an assembly of mitered dividers to house the drawers. What I really like about this feature is that it allows you to finish out an interior space after the case is constructed. Essentially, I create an inte-

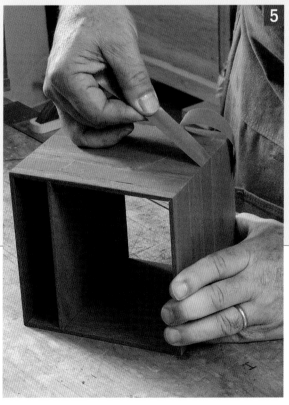

SIZING A SLIDING DOOR

Adding a sliding door to a case is not difficult, but you do need to plan ahead. A full-size drawing will help with the groove placement, and a test piece will help you size the door before you trim the real thing.

The first step is to cut the door grooves in the case before glue-up. Make the lower groove as shallow as possible, no more than 1/16 in. deep, and the top groove deep enough to tilt the door into place, usually 1/4 in. deep (**1**). This allows a longer tab on the top of the door to fit into the groove, while a shallow tab rests in the bottom groove. Use a push pad and a flat-top blade (**2**) or router bit to cut the grooves.

Next, make a test piece to size the door. If you start with the real thing, you can end up with a door that's too narrow or with top and bottom rails of the wrong size once you get the door to fit. Cut the strip to approximate length and rabbet the ends to create tabs to fit in the case grooves. The width of the tabs should be slightly less than the groove width. Make the lower tab 1/8 in. long. This will create a 1/16-in. shadow line at the bottom of the door. Cut the upper tab roughly 3/16 in. to 1/4 in. long, and bevel the rear corner to allow it to be tilted into place (**3**). It needs to be short enough to tilt into place, but long enough so that it doesn't fall out of the groove once installed (**4**). It will take a little trial and error to get the fit just right so that the door fits into place with as little of a gap as possible at the top. Use the test piece to size the actual door, which allows you to take the tabs into consideration when determining the width of the upper and lower rails.

The through-dovetails made cutting the joinery a little easier, but 10 drawers is still a lot of drawers.

rior lining to the box that I can outfit with a series of horizontal and vertical dividers. These can be very thin—1/4 in. or even less—so the look doesn't get too heavy.

The outer border of the divider assembly is similar to a mitered box. But because the stock is much thinner than a typical box, I use a V-groove router bit to cut the miters rather than the tablesaw miter jig I used for the mitered tea box earlier (see p. 121). I join the dividers to the border and to each other with a bird's-mouth joint, with a point on one part fitting into a V-groove in the other. To make the grooves and miters, I used the same bit I used for the miters. To fine-tune the length of the mitered parts, I made a simple shooting board. Rather than attempt to hold the stock at a 45° angle to plane the end, the workpiece sits flat on the jig while an angled fence supports the plane at 45° in order to make the cut. The advantage of this type of joint over a standard dado joint is that the front edges of the dividers can be profiled and the transitions from part to part will be seamless. To keep the parts aligned and to prevent gaps at the corners, I glued up the dividers into a single unit and then slid it back into the case.

I waited until the dividers were in place before sizing the drawer parts. The through-dovetails made cutting the joinery a little easier, but 10 drawers is still a lot of drawers. The good news is that your dovetailing skills will be a little sharper once you're finished.

CARVE AN INSET FOR THE DRAWER PULLS

A coved recess allows the pulls to be inset far enough to clear the door and still let you get a grip on them. Drill three holes at each pull location: a through hole for the pull, a deeper hole with a slightly larger diameter than the post hole to establish the bottom of the recess, and a shallow ¾-in. hole to establish the perimeter (**1**). It takes just a few minutes to carve a hollow between the outer rim and the bottom of the recess (**2**). Make sure to smooth the transitions and remove any hard edges between the drilled holes and the carved hollow (**3**).

A STEP FORWARD
OR MAYBE TO THE SIDE

Like the Moon jewelry chest, this piece also has its genesis in a leftover dovetail demo prop. Kumiko makes an appearance as well, along with a new addition to my design arsenal: a live-edge base. Like the Moon chest, this piece is called for a sliding door, but there were some significant differences between the two projects. Kumiko had become a frequent feature in my work by the time I started in on this chest, and I had begun to get interested in the finer points of tea and creating pieces to house tea ware—teapots and cups and such. But before I could get started on this particular piece I needed to get an idea of what types of items would need to be stored. It turns out the answer wasn't that simple. Depending on the origin, the type of tea, and the brewing method, the tea ware required is all over the map. A little frustrating at first, but ultimately it was a good thing in that it would be a while before I could exhaust the possibilities.

THE RITUAL OF TEA

All this, of course, necessitated my becoming reacquainted with drinking teas. Japanese green teas, Chinese red teas, Taiwanese oolongs. The one thing they all have in common is that the brewing of the tea is as much a part of the process as the drinking of the tea. This is true when using even a simple tea bag. There is an element of time intrinsic to tea, and those few minutes that it takes to brew can offer a respite from the chaos of a typical day. Because of that there is a ritualistic quality to the experience, and every piece of tea ware, from a tea jar to a bamboo scoop to a teapot and tea cup, informs that ritual, that experience. There is also an opportunity for woodwork to play a role in that as well. So a box for tea, a shelf for pots and cups, and a chest to be brought to a table can all add to the experience.

There is also the opportunity to combine wood with other materials. The matte black textures of a cast-iron teapot and the bubbling glazes of a rough-hewn tea bowl contrast and complement woodwork in an amazing way. It's odd that as perfect and pristine as I try to make my work, my favorite ceramics are those that are the most misshapen and "flawed." I find that as different in nature as they are, they tend to get along best with my work, elevating it to a different level. I realized that a piece of woodwork doesn't need to be complete in itself, that it can play just a part in a richer harmony. It was a humbling yet reassuring thought.

Rather than being conceived as a jewelry chest, this piece was a tea chest from the start. I had originally intended to house tea ware inside of the chest, but the idea of concealing objects that were better off on display bothered me a little. Instead, I stumbled on the

A TWO-STILE SOLUTION

The tea chest door is wider than it is tall. Creating a square opening for the kumiko panel resulted in stiles that were much wider than the rails, which made the door look odd and clunky. To solve the problem, I split each wide stile into a pair of narrower stiles. Not only did this solve the problem of the wide stile, but it also introduced a nice visual element to the chest. The stiles are joined with stub tenons that fit into grooves in the rails. This made it easy to position the stiles during glue-up. I used the kumiko panel itself to set the distance between the inner stiles, and inserted shims between the inner and outer stiles for even spacing.

idea of placing a smaller chest on a longer shelf or base. When I sat a leftover dovetailed case on a random board on my bench, I knew there was something to the idea. To figure out the partitioning of the chest, I drew combinations of drawers and doors on cardboard and placed them in the opening of the case. To get a sense of how the scale of the chest would work with a tea set, out came a pot and cups from the kitchen (right). This was not a stroke of creative genius, this was play. And it was fun. In a nutshell, this process captured the core of what drives my work today. Play. Fun. Whimsy. Discovery. Glimpsing a spark of an idea and chasing it down to a finished piece. Bringing that wisp of a thought into the real world, having someone look at it and say "oh," with a sense of familiarity and discovery at the same time: That's what gets me into the shop every day and sustains me through sharpening sessions and emptying the dust collector.

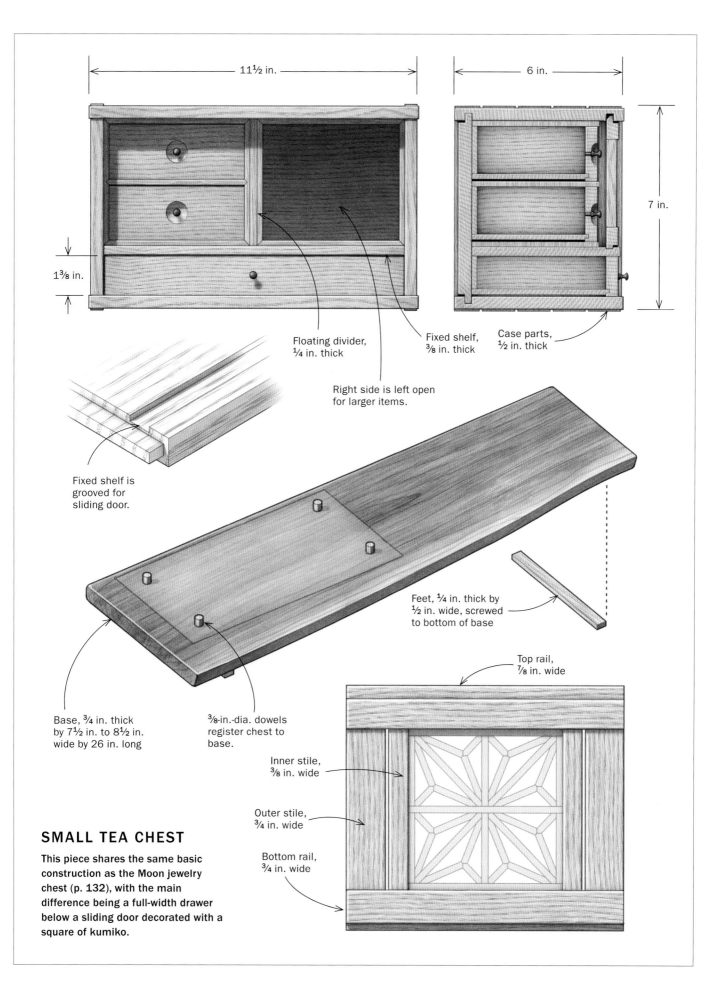

11½ in.

6 in.

7 in.

1⅜ in.

Floating divider,
¼ in. thick

Fixed shelf,
⅜ in. thick

Case parts,
½ in. thick

Right side is left open
for larger items.

Fixed shelf is
grooved for
sliding door.

Base, ¾ in. thick
by 7½ in. to 8½ in.
wide by 26 in. long

⅜-in.-dia. dowels
register chest to
base.

Feet, ¼ in. thick by
½ in. wide, screwed
to bottom of base

Top rail,
⅞ in. wide

Inner stile,
⅜ in. wide

Outer stile,
¾ in. wide

Bottom rail,
¾ in. wide

SMALL TEA CHEST

This piece shares the same basic
construction as the Moon jewelry
chest (p. 132), with the main
difference being a full-width drawer
below a sliding door decorated with a
square of kumiko.

A CHEST DISGUISED AS A BOX

S o what would happen if you built a chest with a folding, sliding door and filled it with shelves, but then flipped it on its back? And added rope handles. And then filled it with tea packets. I guess you'd have a box. I originally planned on including a section on boxes and another on chests. They were different things in my mind and I liked each for different reasons. But when I took a look at what I wanted to include in each section, I had a hard time deciding where each piece belonged.

Once again, this project began with a leftover from a dovetail demo. I actually tried ebonizing it at some point. I sanded it back to bare wood, but remnants of black still live in the dovetails. I took a wire brush to the surface and waxed it without a finish. It was an odd shape that had taken a lot of experimental abuse, and I'm a little amazed that it escaped the wood stove. My first thought was to make it a chest, but the proportions were a little too tall and shallow. Instead I laid it flat and called it a box.

The lid was the biggest challenge, and it ended up defining the piece. I initially didn't want hinges (though I ended up with some anyway), and I didn't want a lift-off lid on a box that large, as I'd always be trying to find a place to put it. It wasn't deep enough for a pair of sliding lids, and a single sliding lid didn't make a lot of sense. So a sliding, hinged lid somehow bubbled up from those thoughts. There are full-length grooves in the case sides and grooves along the edges of one of the lid panels. Splines glued into the grooves in the lid panel allow it to slide back and forth.

The other panel has a handle on one end that rests in a notch on the case end. You lift one half of the lid to access one side of the box and slide the folded panels over to get to the other half. Walnut dividers keep everything organized. Amazingly, the proportions are just right for the contents. I always look for a reason to add rope handles to anything (see p. 155 for how to install them), and the size of this box provided the opportunity. It's one thing to drag out a cardboard box of tea packets from the cupboard for company, but carrying a handmade chest to the table sets the stage for a nice tea party.

It wasn't deep enough for a pair of sliding lids, and a single sliding lid didn't make a lot of sense. So a sliding, hinged lid somehow bubbled up from those thoughts.

CHAPTER 6

CASEWORK

I use *casework* as a loose term for pieces that sit on the floor and hold things—anything that you neither eat at, sit on (for the most part), or hang from a wall. That covers quite a lot. It represents much of what we build and much of what we need for our homes. A sideboard, a bookcase, a bedroom dresser. Shelves, doors, drawers. The combinations are even more varied than those of a wall cabinet, in that scale and function hold so many more possibilities. Every furniture style has its quintessential casework piece: the Queen Anne highboy, the Federal serpentine sideboard, the Arts and Crafts sideboard, and the Shaker tall cupboard.

If you want to build furniture, you can pretty much start with casework and end with casework and never get bored in between. In this chapter, you'll find many of the forms that casework can assume, including cases with solid sides (or slab construction), and frame-and-panel casework, which can pose more challenges but offers more versatility as well. And finally, I couldn't leave out one of my favorite forms: the case on stand.

ONE SHOE BENCH BEGETS ANOTHER

While I've always tried to build furniture to last a long time, this piece opened my eyes to the notion of a piece having a long useful life as well.

One of the most important milestones along my woodworking journey is an unassuming little piece that I built when I moved to Connecticut with my wife and infant son to begin work at *Fine Woodworking* magazine (photo at left). At the time, I was faced with a storage dilemma. We had a TV and a VCR (remember those?) and a little cabinet that was too small for both to fit on. I ran to Home Depot and grabbed a 1×12 board, cut it into three pieces, and joined everything together with crude protruding dovetails. The stand went on the cabinet, and the TV sat on top while the VCR was tucked underneath. I never did glue the parts together.

After its stint as a TV shelf, the piece migrated to the bathroom, where our kids used it as a step to reach the faucet. It served as a shoe bench for the kids as well. When they had outgrown it, the well-traveled piece headed to the basement, where it lived next to the washing machine and served as a nice platform to set laundry baskets on. I believe, at the moment, it may reside under a TV in the basement once again, this time making room for a video-game console. It never did get a finish either, so it ended up acquiring a, shall we say, "rich" patina of use. It wears its age well though, and has seen 20 years of regular use. While I've always tried to build furniture to last a long time, this piece opened my eyes to the notion of a piece having a long useful life as well.

This basic form has inspired many case pieces that followed, and my hope is that a little of its vitality has been passed along.

MORE SHOE BENCHES FOLLOW

The next shoe bench I built had the same dovetailed corners as well as an added shelf. Because it's a piece that you interact with, the proud dovetails become not just a visual detail but a tactile one as well. It's an idea that began to inform future pieces. The bench was made from thick white oak boards for a solid stance (left). A slight arched chamfer along the bottom edge of the shelf lightened the look just a little and gave the piece a slight spring in its stance. When a piece is so linear, just the slightest curve can add a nice pop. A valuable lesson learned and another tool added to my design kit.

I was left with a bench that looked a little clunky and top heavy. I addressed the problem by dividing the center drawer into two shallower stacked drawers.

Finally, a larger shoe bench expanded on this idea. I borrowed the basic form from the earlier benches but made it longer and higher. Then I filled out the upper portion with drawers for winter hats and mittens. I built the drawers nice and deep for lots of storage, but I was left with a bench that looked a little clunky and top heavy. I addressed the problem by dividing the center drawer into two shallower stacked drawers. I think it worked pretty well and now we have a place for computer and notebook paper, though one less drawer for winter clutter.

For the pulls I turned to iron hardware, which is most likely an echo of the hand-hammered hardware I would use on Arts and Crafts work. Hardware is one of those things that's tough to get right, especially if you leave it as an afterthought. Whether simple or ornate, the hardware you choose will have a big impact on the look of the piece. I tend to be pretty conservative in my hardware choices, using the same style over and over again. Like anything else, when working with something often enough you can anticipate the effect it will have and you can begin to design with it in mind. The bookcase that follows on p. 152 is very similar in construction, but its wrapped handles take it in a different direction.

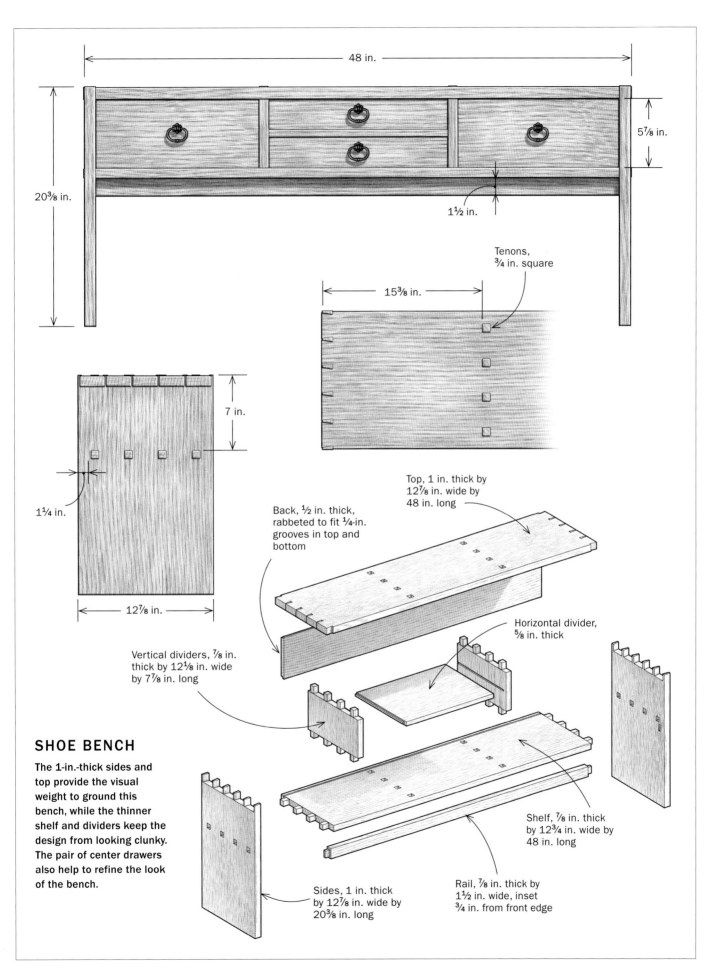

48 in.

5⁷⁄₈ in.

20³⁄₈ in.

1¹⁄₂ in.

Tenons,
³⁄₄ in. square

15³⁄₈ in.

7 in.

1¹⁄₄ in.

12⁷⁄₈ in.

Top, 1 in. thick by
12⁷⁄₈ in. wide by
48 in. long

Back, ¹⁄₂ in. thick,
rabbeted to fit ¹⁄₄-in.
grooves in top and
bottom

Horizontal divider,
⁵⁄₈ in. thick

Vertical dividers, ⁷⁄₈ in.
thick by 12¹⁄₈ in. wide
by 7⁷⁄₈ in. long

SHOE BENCH

The 1-in.-thick sides and
top provide the visual
weight to ground this
bench, while the thinner
shelf and dividers keep the
design from looking clunky.
The pair of center drawers
also help to refine the look
of the bench.

Shelf, ⁷⁄₈ in. thick
by 12³⁄₄ in. wide by
48 in. long

Sides, 1 in. thick
by 12⁷⁄₈ in. wide by
20³⁄₈ in. long

Rail, ⁷⁄₈ in. thick by
1¹⁄₂ in. wide, inset
³⁄₄ in. from front edge

A NEAR MISS DOESN'T HAVE TO GO TO WASTE

If something can perform its function well and add a little personality to the surroundings, that's not such a bad thing.

A brandy cabinet took the shoe bench idea to new heights (lower left). It actually holds seltzer (that's East Coast speak for sparkling water), as well as leftover paper birthday napkins and mouse traps. It sits in the corner of our kitchen and definitely earns its keep. However, it suffers from the fatal flaw of being made from stock that is too thin. At least I think that's what the problem is.

It was a little tough to include a piece that I'm not truly happy with, but I wanted to keep things real. I tried addressing the flaw by adding oversize tusk tenons to the bottom shelf. The idea was to add some visual mass to the lower section of the cabinet where the thin sides were most evident. Unfortunately, it just looks as though I added a big tusk tenon to a cabinet. While tusk tenons are not bad in and of themselves—and I've seen wonderful examples of furniture that makes good use of them—they have to be something that you plan into a piece rather than tack on as a fix. Later, I even added caps to the feet, which can be cool as well, but it still doesn't sit right for me.

These types of near misses are frustrating, but living with one everyday is a reminder to get the details right in the first place. While I don't admonish myself for it, there is a sense of unfinished business whenever I look at the cabinet. It's not so much that I have a need to fix this piece, but I do want to put its lessons to use to somehow pay tribute to what it was meant to be. This may sound as though I'm ready to throw it on a bonfire, but in spite of its shortcomings, it's a piece that serves a purpose well. That in itself is a good reminder that inasmuch as we may strive for perfection in every aspect of what we make, if something can perform its function well and add a little personality to the surroundings, that's not such a bad thing.

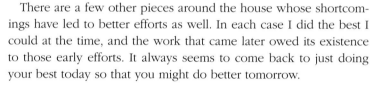

There are a few other pieces around the house whose shortcomings have led to better efforts as well. In each case I did the best I could at the time, and the work that came later owed its existence to those early efforts. It always seems to come back to just doing your best today so that you might do better tomorrow.

A BOOKCASE OFFERED A SECOND CHANCE

This small bookcase benefitted from the lessons learned from the brandy cabinet. It sits by my Morris chair in the TV room, and its upper shelf serves as a nice perch for remotes and such. It's a happy little piece that fits its corner well.

This time around, I started with thicker stock. I also sized the piece a little smaller than a typical bookcase. The combination of those choices resulted in a stout little case that doesn't feel overpowering. Instead of a raised lower shelf like the one on the brandy cabinet, the lower shelf on the bookcase is positioned just off the floor with a narrow apron below it, which also helps to ground the piece. There's another difference between the two pieces that goes beyond getting the details right, however. When making the brandy cabinet, I was struggling to get a sense of what I wanted the piece to be throughout the entire building process. I had made a quick mock-up but jumped into building before it was really resolved. So when it wasn't working, I tried various fixes without really knowing which direction I needed to go.

The bookcase, on the other hand, started with a much better idea of what the finished project wanted to be. So when deciding about the scale, stock thickness, and drawer pulls, my focus wasn't on whether they made it look better or worse, but on whether they got me closer to my goal. I was only able to do that because I had a better idea of where the finish line was. One reason for that was that I had some extra lumber on hand. I have a small shop with not much room for long-term lumber storage. As a result, I tend to design first and then buy the lumber to match the design. But while I was on a lumber run for an upcoming project I came across some beautiful white oak boards I couldn't pass up. I had neither the money nor the room for them, but they ended up on my roof racks anyway.

As the boards sat, and as I eased my way around them every day, the idea of a bookcase began to form in my mind. By the time I had picked up a sketchbook, the design had already resolved itself in my mind. I've actually started to trust this type of back-burner design process. I've found that when I have an upcoming project I should be thinking about, sometimes it's best not to, or at least not to think about it directly. Those ideas that have a chance to percolate in the back of my mind as I'm tackling other jobs are the ones that tend to come together more easily once I turn my full attention to them. I found some nice knotty pine for the backboards and made the drawer pulls from wrapped hemp cord, and the construction went smoothly without a lot of second-guessing.

It's a little odd to think of furniture as happy or friendly. Those terms might prompt images of talking-cartoon furniture. Maybe "open" and "inviting" are closer to the point. Either way, this bookcase, along with other current work, feels that way to me. I tend to hit closer to the mark when I start with a clear idea, trust it, and just keep it simple. Happy little furniture, it could be worse.

BOOKCASE WITH DRAWERS

This small bookcase isn't too far removed from a classic Arts and Crafts piece. Dovetails at the top corners and wrapped cord handles take it in a slightly different direction though.

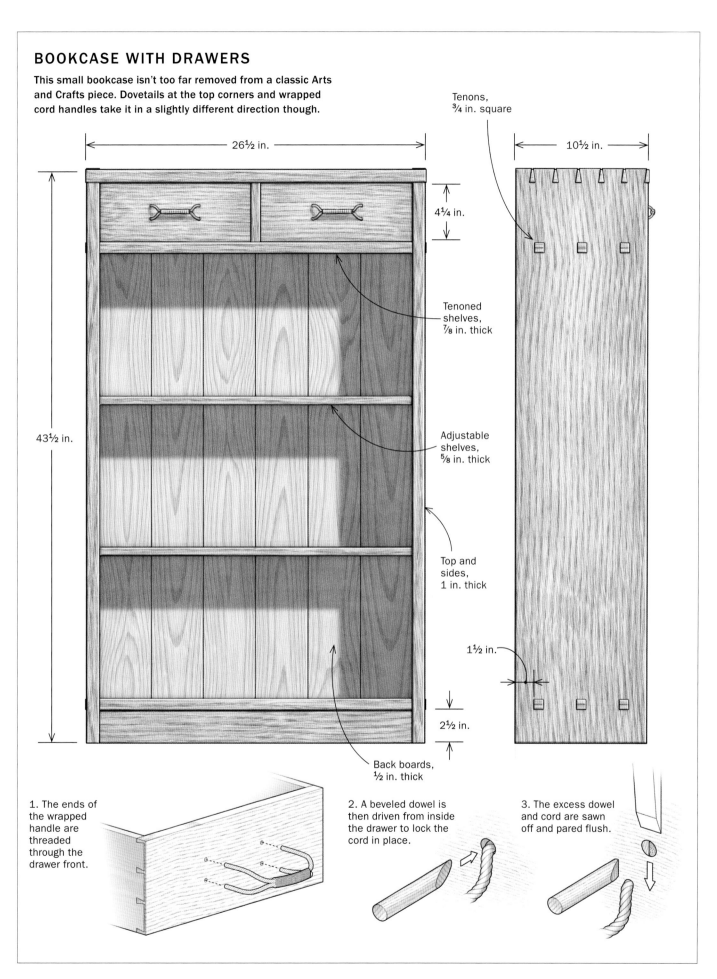

26½ in.

Tenons, ¾ in. square

10½ in.

4¼ in.

Tenoned shelves, ⅞ in. thick

43½ in.

Adjustable shelves, ⅝ in. thick

Top and sides, 1 in. thick

1½ in.

2½ in.

Back boards, ½ in. thick

1. The ends of the wrapped handle are threaded through the drawer front.

2. A beveled dowel is then driven from inside the drawer to lock the cord in place.

3. The excess dowel and cord are sawn off and pared flush.

A LIGHT, LOW DRESSER

The idea was to get away from the boxy look typical of dressers, so I started with a frame-and-panel design that allowed me to work larger and lighter than slab construction would.

The Smith Lake dresser is named after a small lake in the Sierras we used to hike to for picnics. That's neither here nor there, but I've always liked the idea of naming pieces, though I could never come up with anything particularly interesting or meaningful. But this name seemed to fit because the design feels more akin to the California mountains than the hills of Connecticut.

In designing the dresser, I decided to add some subtle curves to an otherwise Arts and Crafts–inspired design. The idea was to get away from the boxy look typical of dressers, so I started with a frame-and-panel design that allowed me to work larger and lighter than slab construction would. I also added legs to give the dresser a lift off the ground, but when supporting such a large mass on legs, the piece was at risk of looking a little top heavy. To help ground it and give it a more solid stance, I decided to widen the legs at the bottom. Rather than the more typical concave bell-bottom curve where the feet would flare out at the base, I went with a slight convex curve. The idea was to widen the legs with something more interesting than a straight taper, but not draw too much attention to the curve.

DETAILS THAT DEFINE THE DRESSER

The next task was to add a little visual interest where the case meets the top. Here, I borrowed an idea from the apron on a hayrake table I had built earlier (see p. 192). The apron fit into a haunch on the top of the legs and extended beyond them where a curved cutout created the look of a corbel. Because the corbel is a common detail in the Arts and Crafts style, I figured it could work for the dresser as well. At this point, I liked where the design was headed, but the simple rectangular top with square edges was looking a little clunky. So I added a slight curve to the ends and a slight radius to the edge profile.

Along the face of the dresser, I incorporated the familiar offsets between the parts. The effect isn't evident on the drawings, but it did create some nice shadows and

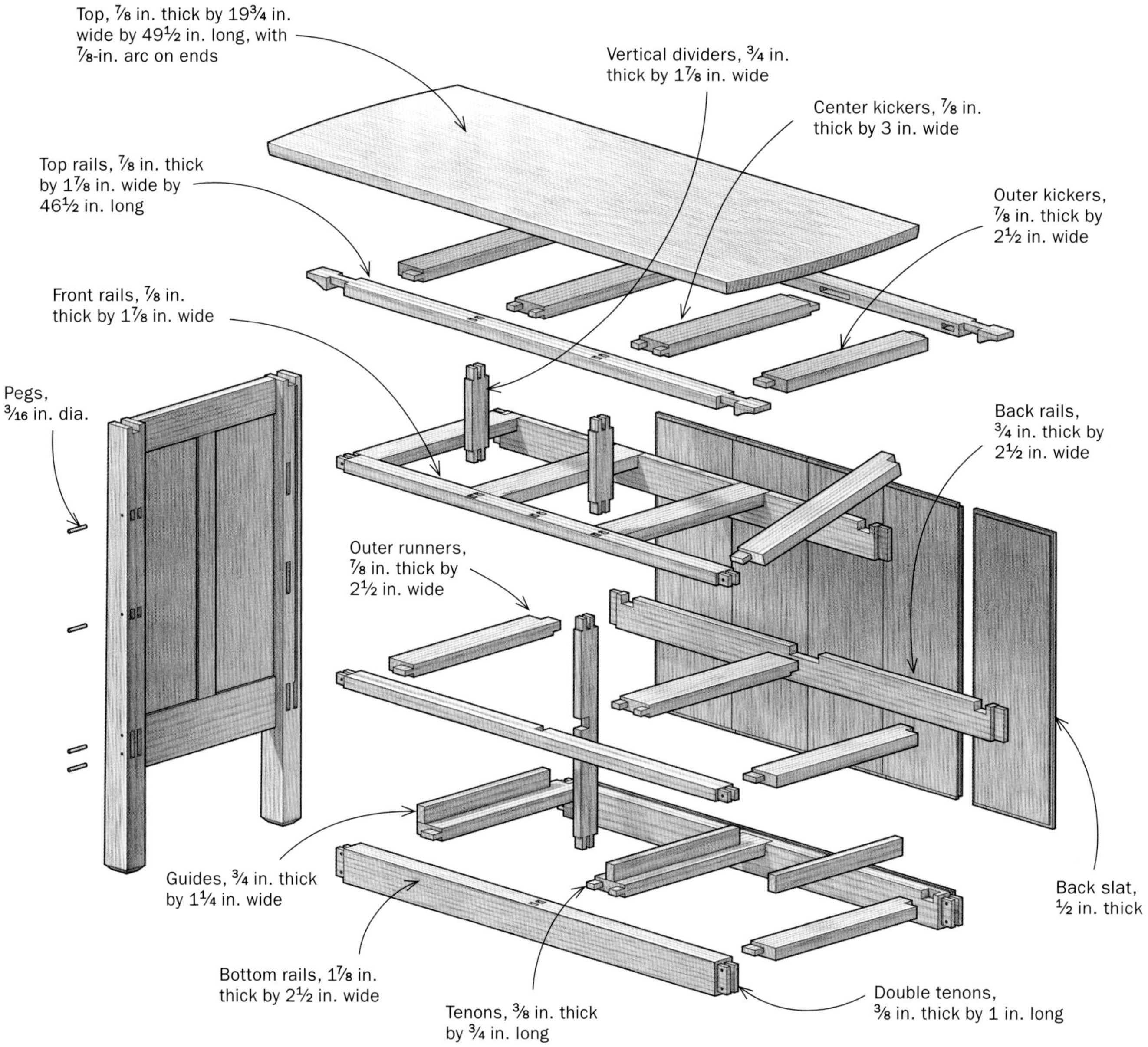
Top, 7/8 in. thick by 19 3/4 in. wide by 49 1/2 in. long, with 7/8-in. arc on ends
Vertical dividers, 3/4 in. thick by 1 7/8 in. wide
Center kickers, 7/8 in. thick by 3 in. wide
Top rails, 7/8 in. thick by 1 7/8 in. wide by 46 1/2 in. long
Outer kickers, 7/8 in. thick by 2 1/2 in. wide
Front rails, 7/8 in. thick by 1 7/8 in. wide
Pegs, 3/16 in. dia.
Back rails, 3/4 in. thick by 2 1/2 in. wide
Outer runners, 7/8 in. thick by 2 1/2 in. wide
Guides, 3/4 in. thick by 1 1/4 in. wide
Back slat, 1/2 in. thick
Bottom rails, 1 7/8 in. thick by 2 1/2 in. wide
Tenons, 3/8 in. thick by 3/4 in. long
Double tenons, 3/8 in. thick by 1 in. long

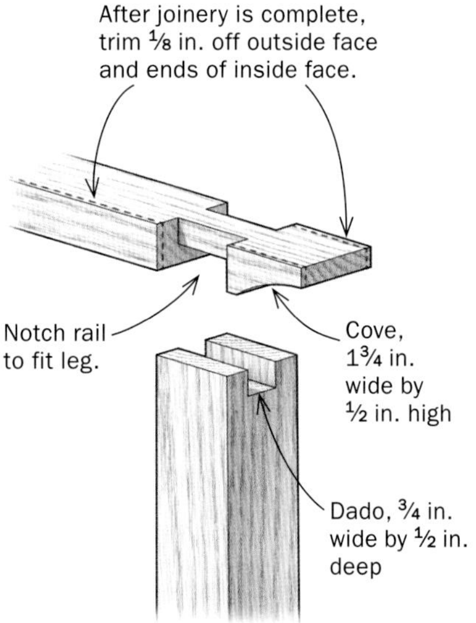
After joinery is complete, trim 1/8 in. off outside face and ends of inside face.
Notch rail to fit leg.
Cove, 1 3/4 in. wide by 1/2 in. high
Dado, 3/4 in. wide by 1/2 in. deep

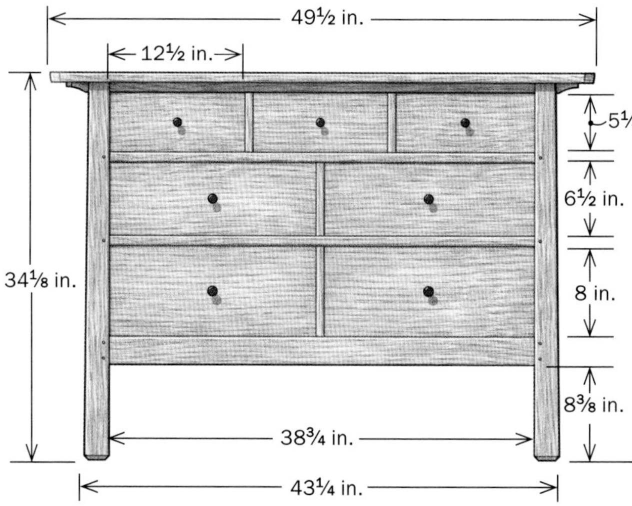
49 1/2 in.
12 1/2 in.
34 1/8 in.
5 1/4 in.
6 1/2 in.
8 in.
8 3/8 in.
38 3/4 in.
43 1/4 in.

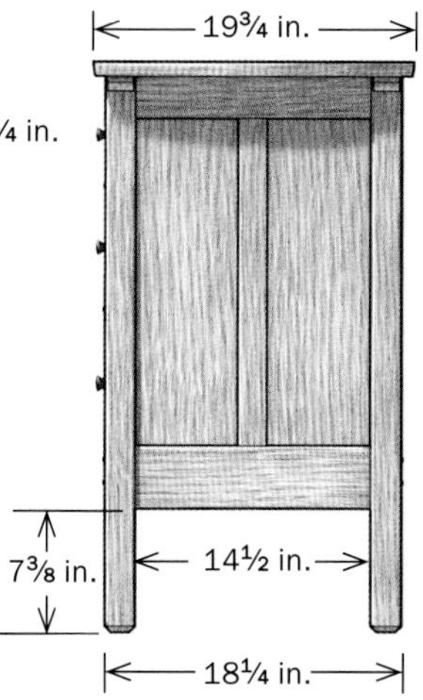
19 3/4 in.
7 3/8 in.
14 1/2 in.
18 1/4 in.

LOW DRESSER

The white oak legs and frame add strength to this dresser, while butternut panels and drawer fronts soften the look and lighten the load.

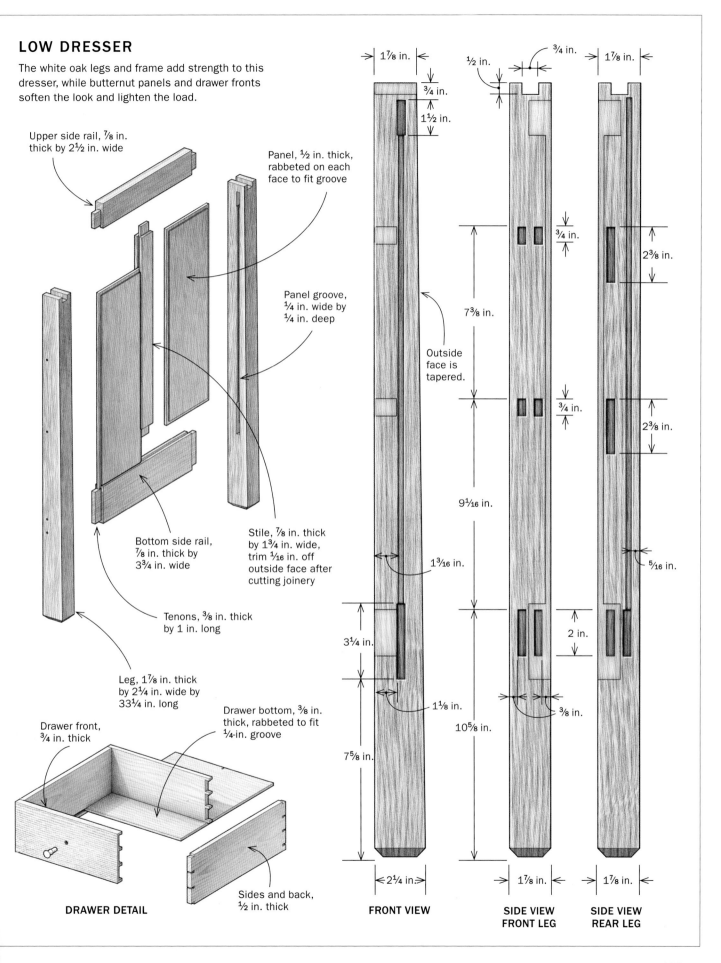

Upper side rail, ⁷⁄₈ in. thick by 2½ in. wide

Panel, ½ in. thick, rabbeted on each face to fit groove

Panel groove, ¼ in. wide by ¼ in. deep

Bottom side rail, ⁷⁄₈ in. thick by 3¾ in. wide

Stile, ⁷⁄₈ in. thick by 1¾ in. wide, trim ¹⁄₁₆ in. off outside face after cutting joinery

Tenons, ⅜ in. thick by 1 in. long

Leg, 1⁷⁄₈ in. thick by 2¼ in. wide by 33¼ in. long

Drawer front, ¾ in. thick

Drawer bottom, ⅜ in. thick, rabbeted to fit ¼-in. groove

Sides and back, ½ in. thick

DRAWER DETAIL

1⁷⁄₈ in.

¾ in.

1½ in.

7⅜ in.

Outside face is tapered.

9¹⁄₁₆ in.

1³⁄₁₆ in.

3¼ in.

7⅝ in.

2¼ in.

FRONT VIEW

½ in.

¾ in.

1⁷⁄₈ in.

¾ in.

¾ in.

2 in.

⅜ in.

10⅝ in.

1⅛ in.

1⁷⁄₈ in.

SIDE VIEW FRONT LEG

2⅜ in.

2⅜ in.

⁵⁄₁₆ in.

1⁷⁄₈ in.

SIDE VIEW REAR LEG

BRIDLE JOINTS AT THE TOP

Instead of dovetailing the top rails to the legs, I notched them to fit dadoes in the legs. The overhanging ends of the rails are then coved to create a nice design detail. After mortising the legs, I dadoed their tops using a tenoning jig at the tablesaw (**1**). Then I notched the outside corners at the bandsaw to create a flat shoulder for the top rail to seat in (**2**). This allowed me to shape the outside of the legs without affecting the fit (**3**). I used a pair of stops at the tablesaw to notch the top rails (**4**). Leaving the stops in place, I first removed most of the waste at the bandsaw and then slid the rail back and forth between the stops to create the final profile (**5**). Finally, I cut the profile on the rail ends at the bandsaw, and then used the off-cut as a sanding block to smooth the shape (**6**). Once the first end on the first rail was cut, I used that as a template for tracing out the remaining corbels.

It wasn't a matter of thinking of woods in terms of color, but in terms of what the nature of each wood would lend to the other.

highlights along the front to keep it from looking like a single slab of drawer fronts and stretchers.

Choosing lumber for the dresser was a challenge as well. While the design has a definite Arts and Crafts feel, which would typically call for quartersawn oak, it didn't seem quite right for this piece because it would dominate the dresser. I did like the idea of riftsawn oak for the legs, frame, and stretchers, where its quieter, straight grain would add both visual order and perceived strength to the case. For the panels and drawer fronts, though, butternut with its softer shimmer kept coming to mind. Both woods are almost identical in color and tone, which made the final result a little hard to visualize, and I worried that it might look too bland.

What really drove the idea was my intuitive response to each wood from having worked with them for a while. I had an idea of how the woods would complement each other: oak with its weight, mass, and permanence, and butternut with its glow and iridescent sheen. It wasn't a matter of thinking of woods in terms of color, but in terms of what the nature of each wood would lend to the other, and I decided just to trust it. In the end, I think the pairing was successful. It's a piece I live with and it's something I notice (in a good way) every time I look at it. It's a choice I probably wouldn't have made had I not worked with each wood long enough to have an understanding of them.

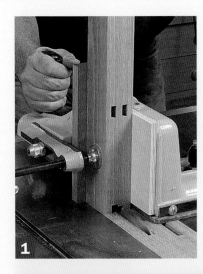

BREAK DOWN THE CASE ASSEMBLY

The dresser has a lot of parts, and gluing them up all at once would be a nightmare. So after I prefinished all of the parts with a thin coat of shellac, I glued up the case in stages.

Start by gluing up the side assemblies (**1**). Once the glue is dry and the clamps are off, connect the sides by adding the front-rail assembly and rear rails in between (**2**). To avoid having to glue in the drawer guides at the same time, the rear rails are notched so that they can tilt into place afterward (**3**). The next step is to slide the tongue-and-groove back panels into place (**4**), and then cap off the base by fitting the top-rail assembly into place (**5**).

It's a few steps, but none of them are particularly stressful, and the benefit of breaking down assembly into so many parts outweighs having to wait for the glue to dry between steps. The last task is to add the drawer guides. Use a combination square to align the guides with the vertical dividers and to make sure they are square to the front of the case (**6**). If they're off, it will make drawer fitting more difficult than it needs to be.

1

Sometimes the things that I'm most excited about in a finished piece are the aspects that are never seen at all.

The actual construction of the dresser is relatively straightforward. If you can cut a mortise-and-tenon joint and run a groove and rabbet, you can build the case without a problem. If you have your dovetails down, the drawers will come together easily enough as well. The one joint that might be new to you is where the top rails meet the legs. It's a simple joint and is one of the keys to the dresser's personality.

Another challenge that had me scratching my head for a while was how to go about getting everything assembled once the joinery was cut. The solution I finally settled on was to glue up the sides first, and then break down the rest of the assembly into multiple steps. This approach took the stress out of an otherwise complicated glue-up. It turned out that the assembly method actually dictated aspects of the joinery of the case, too. Fortunately, I had been preoccupied with the challenge of bringing everything together from the outset. As I began to settle on a path, I was able to choose construction methods to suit it. I had found a way to install the drawer supports after the fact, and I added internal rear rails that allowed the back boards to be installed later as well.

For me, it was a really good reminder that thinking a project through from beginning to end before reaching for a piece of lumber is, well, a really good idea. While we usually fall into the habit of thinking of design in visual terms, the engineering of a piece—figuring out how it all goes together and where the strength is coming from—is actually a much bigger and more important part of the design puzzle to solve. Sometimes the things that I'm most excited about in a finished piece are the aspects that are never seen at all.

A CABINET 30 YEARS IN THE MAKING

If I had known how long it would take to make simple work, I might not have begun the journey.

I've always worked with voices in my head: Mentors, critics, teachers, and clients all have a say in the work I try to do. One particular voice has always been kind, gentle, encouraging, and understanding of the long journey toward simplicity. I first read James Krenov when I was a college student. His words tapped into the psyche of a struggling artist and furniture maker looking for a voice and a path. His words coaxed me forward, but his work was the real inspiration: simple work, humble in its way, but alive. It added power to his words and provided a direct connection between the philosophy with which you work and the resulting product. It's no coincidence that this is a driving theme throughout my work. One of Krenov's favorite foils was the cabinet on stand, a simple form that offered endless variety and endless challenge. The piece is almost a rite of passage for the students at the College of the Redwoods, where he held court for years. It was a piece that I, too, had wanted to tackle from the first time I saw his work.

So why has it taken me so long to get to it? I can't say for sure, but it's probably a good thing that it has. I benefitted from just about all of the knowledge and experience I've acquired in the intervening years to tackle the project. Simple is hard. And

ignorance, I'm told, is bliss. Or at least a blessing, in that if I had known how long it would take to make simple work, I might not have begun the journey.

The inspiration for this piece was a chance meeting with a wonderful bird carver. I discovered Jane Layton's work at a photo seminar I was giving at a crafts guild in Lexington, Mass. The birds were carved and painted jewels of realism, and Jane was diminutive and soft-spoken with sparkling eyes. I was between commissions and classes at the time, so I proposed a trade: a pair of cardinals as an anniversary present for my wife in exchange for a piece of furniture. I suggested a display case for her carvings and asked what style and wood she would like it in. "I like your work, you know what you're doing, you decide." The idea of a cabinet on stand immediately sprang to mind—a light, delicate case, pristine.

I felt some intimidation at the thought of tackling a Krenov-inspired piece. At this point in my journey, I'd worked in various styles—Arts and Crafts, Shaker, Queen Anne, Federal—but in making this piece, I didn't want to merely work in the "Krenov style" as if it were another hat to try on. So I stopped and reminded myself to come as myself to the party, to try to work from a more authentic place. That meant a dovetailed cabinet and proud tenons for the stand. I chose white oak for the stand, but went with ash for the cabinet. Ash is a pale wood, but with strong grain that's an equal match for the oak. I bought wide plain-sawn boards and took just the rift-sawn outer edges for the case. A glue joint at the center is almost invisible and a small price for the straight grain.

For the stand, I also started with a wide, thick oak board and took the parts from the outer edges where the grain dove at an angle, yielding tight, straight grain on every face. Through-joinery connected the base, but I made the tenons a little narrower than usual and varied their lengths. There were proud pins as well, and the result is a fun constellation of dots and dashes. The legs needed just a hint of a curve, but a bandsawn curve was too much. Instead, I relied on a tapered chamfer on the outside corner

of the legs to suggest just a gentle curve to the contour. I added a tapered chamfer at the top of the leg as well. Once I moved away from square parts, I began to consider each aspect, from curves to chamfers to end treatments, and the design possibilities opened up. It was the same feeling I'd had when I began to really pay attention to wood grain in a piece; once my eyes were open to it, I couldn't ignore it anymore.

The base needed to provide solid support for the cabinet, but I wanted to make it look as light as possible. The solution was to break up the rails on each side of the base. I used a pair of aprons on the front and back of the case. The narrower doubled aprons offer the same resistance to racking that a single, wide apron would, but without the visual weight. I lightened the look of the lower apron even further by giving it a subtle arch. On the sides I used single aprons, set down low. Underneath the case, a pair of rails connects the front and back aprons. These two rails add strength to the base and also support and elevate the case, making it appear to float. The construction results in a delicate-looking base that still offers a solid foundation for the case.

A SUBTLE CURVE TO THE LEGS

The base parts were taken from the outer edges of a wide board where the grain ran diagonal to the face and edge (1). Once the joinery has been cut, saw a taper on the outside faces of the legs (2). To suggest a slight curve to the legs, plane a tapered chamfer on the outside corners (3). The chamfer is widest about one third of the way down from the top (4), which creates the impression that the leg tapers from wider at the base to narrower at the top, with the upper section flaring out just a bit. It's a detail that adds a little lift and grace to the piece—something that you might not consciously notice, but somehow you'd miss it if it wasn't there.

The top of the legs has a curve as well. Start with a heavy, even chamfer all the way around. Then plane a subtle curve from the base of the outside chamfer to the top of the inside chamfer (5). This gentle curve also helps to accentuate the flare of the legs.

A SIMPLE ASH CABINET

The cabinet is dovetailed at the corners, and the joinery is left proud and lightly chamfered (**1**). A frame-and-panel back is glued into a rabbet for a cleaner look than screws would provide (**2**). The glass-front door has a simple butternut lattice work to break up the space without blocking the view of the contents (**3**). A square of kumiko made from pine drops into the center section of the butternut grid to add just a little sparkle (**4**).

Small details make a big difference, and there is no end to the possible variations that even a simple form can offer.

The dovetailed cabinet is finished off with a frame-and-panel back that drops into a rabbet in the case. The glass-front door is broken up by a delicate latticework in butternut, its vertical members slightly proud of the horizontals for a hint of a shadow line at the intersections. A kumiko square at the center of the latticework completes the cabinet.

In the end, I was left with the feeling that this piece marked more of a beginning than the end of a journey. Once again, I found that on a simple piece, small details make a big difference, and there is no end to the possible variations that even a simple form can offer. Tackling the cabinet provided an even greater appreciation of Krenov's work, and a sharper eye for the details that played throughout his pieces. The more I look, the more surprises I find. Even after 30 years.

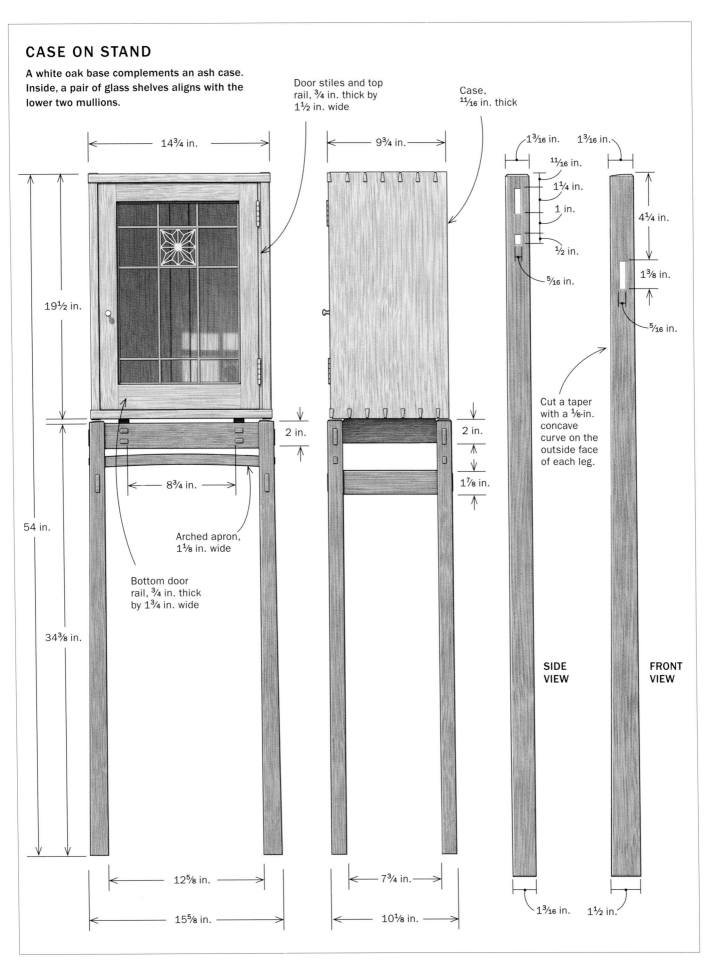

CASE ON STAND

A white oak base complements an ash case. Inside, a pair of glass shelves aligns with the lower two mullions.

Door stiles and top rail, ¾ in. thick by 1½ in. wide

Case, ¹¹⁄₁₆ in. thick

14¾ in.

9¾ in.

1³⁄₁₆ in.   1³⁄₁₆ in.

¹¹⁄₁₆ in.

1¼ in.

1 in.

4¼ in.

19½ in.

½ in.

⁵⁄₁₆ in.

1³⁄₈ in.

⁵⁄₁₆ in.

2 in.

2 in.

Cut a taper with a ⅛-in. concave curve on the outside face of each leg.

8¾ in.

1⅞ in.

Arched apron, 1⅛ in. wide

54 in.

Bottom door rail, ¾ in. thick by 1¾ in. wide

34³⁄₈ in.

SIDE VIEW

FRONT VIEW

12⅝ in.

7¾ in.

15⅝ in.

10⅛ in.

1³⁄₁₆ in.   1½ in.

STATIONERY-INSPIRED NEW YORK ECLECTIC

The Chelsea desk is named for the location of a New York apartment that I visited a few years back. In a living room overstuffed with an amazing assortment of, um, stuff, there was one corner of bare wall that cried out for a small piece to fill it. Something compact, eclectic, utilitarian. Something modern with a resonance of the past. A bookcase? A desk? Multipurpose out of necessity, I supposed.

I started with that list of words. It may seem beside the point, but sometimes words are a better means to sketch out ideas. Often the vague image we can "see" in our minds is really a collection of thoughts and feelings. It sounds weird to think of a design as a thought rather than a picture in our mind but it can be. Not all the words need to be descriptive or directly related to how something should look, but they should convey a feeling or a sense of what you are aiming for. Get them out. Get them down. Let them stew for a while. Let them inform the sketches to follow.

Later, walking past a stationery store, a packet of envelopes and paper provided an inspiration—why not a writing desk? Not for bills or iPads, or laptops, or charging stations, but a desk to pen a letter, with a gallery for stationery and a nook for journals and sketchbooks.

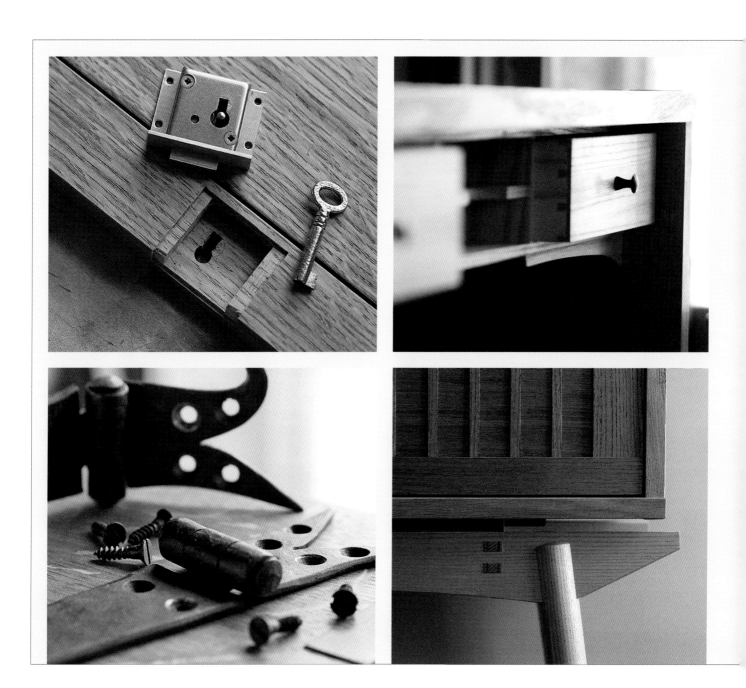

The result was at once familiar and a bit peculiar, in that it utilized elements from previous efforts but combined them in a unique way.

In a way it was a continuation of my thoughts about a cabinet on stand. Whereas my first attempt was firmly tethered to Krenov's influence, I asked myself what one might look like if I were to make it truly my own. The result was at once familiar and a bit peculiar, in that it utilized elements from previous efforts but combined them in a unique way.

The idea of a case on stand with splayed, tapered legs came from a pile of sketches I had made a few years before (see the drawings on p. 30). From there, I borrowed most of the details from recent work: proud dovetails, of course; vertical slats dividing a door panel; a kumiko square for decoration; a long case echoing the Moon jewelry chest; and ash borrowed from the Krenov cabinet.

I was worried that the design wouldn't translate easily or well to real life. It was just a chicken scratch after all, but the vision it provided was clear from the beginning. A mock-up was critical to bringing the idea to life, but the leg splay angles and case size all came together quickly.

A COLLECTION OF FAMILIAR DETAILS

The thing that surprised me about this little desk is that, while most of the elements have shown up in previous work, the end result has a very distinct personality of its own: a dovetailed case, a mix of ash and oak, hand-forged hardware, a door panel with vertical slats, and a square of kumiko to finish it off. It would have been a stretch to think that it would have occurred to me to include all of those elements in a single piece had I not worked with them before. Designing the desk was really a matter of following the stepping-stones left by a number of previous projects. As happy as I was to reach this destination, it's nice to know that it helps to mark the trail toward future projects as well.

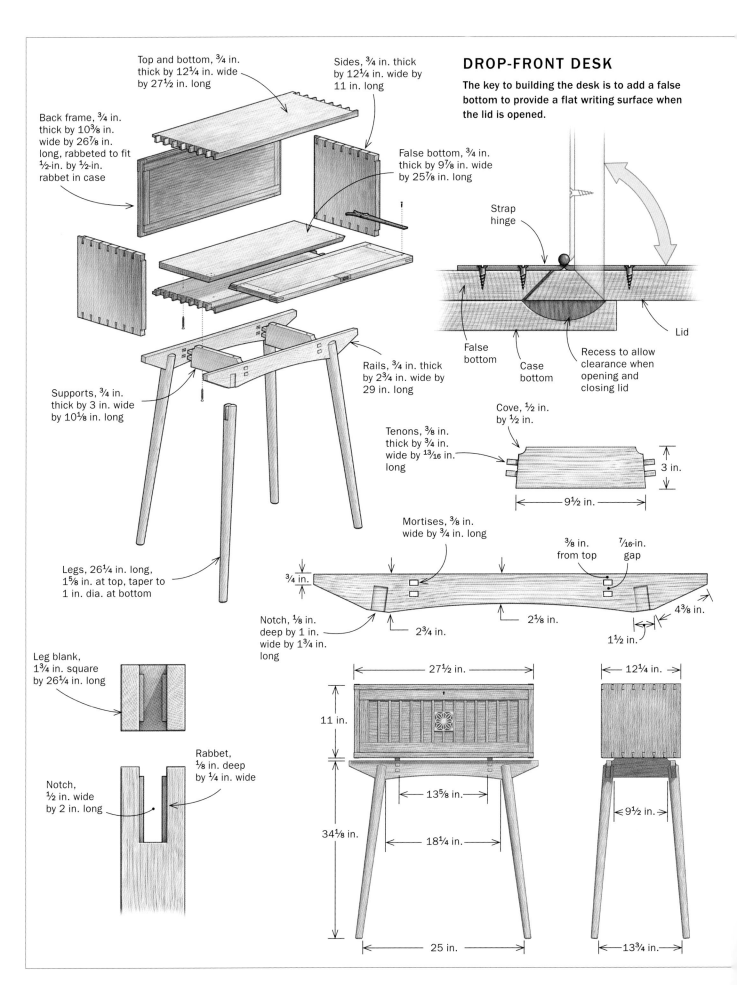

Top and bottom, ¾ in. thick by 12¼ in. wide by 27½ in. long

Sides, ¾ in. thick by 12¼ in. wide by 11 in. long

Back frame, ¾ in. thick by 10⅜ in. wide by 26⅞ in. long, rabbeted to fit ½-in. by ½-in. rabbet in case

False bottom, ¾ in. thick by 9⅞ in. wide by 25⅞ in. long

Supports, ¾ in. thick by 3 in. wide by 10⅛ in. long

Rails, ¾ in. thick by 2¾ in. wide by 29 in. long

Legs, 26¼ in. long, 1⅝ in. at top, taper to 1 in. dia. at bottom

Leg blank, 1¾ in. square by 26¼ in. long

Notch, ½ in. wide by 2 in. long

Rabbet, ⅛ in. deep by ¼ in. wide

DROP-FRONT DESK

The key to building the desk is to add a false bottom to provide a flat writing surface when the lid is opened.

Strap hinge

Lid

False bottom

Case bottom

Recess to allow clearance when opening and closing lid

Cove, ½ in. by ½ in.

Tenons, ⅜ in. thick by ¾ in. wide by 13/16 in. long

3 in.

9½ in.

Mortises, ⅜ in. wide by ¾ in. long

⅜ in. from top

7/16-in. gap

¾ in.

Notch, ⅛ in. deep by 1 in. wide by 1¾ in. long

2¾ in.

2⅛ in.

4⅜ in.

1½ in.

27½ in.

11 in.

34⅛ in.

13⅝ in.

18¼ in.

25 in.

12¼ in.

9½ in.

13¾ in.

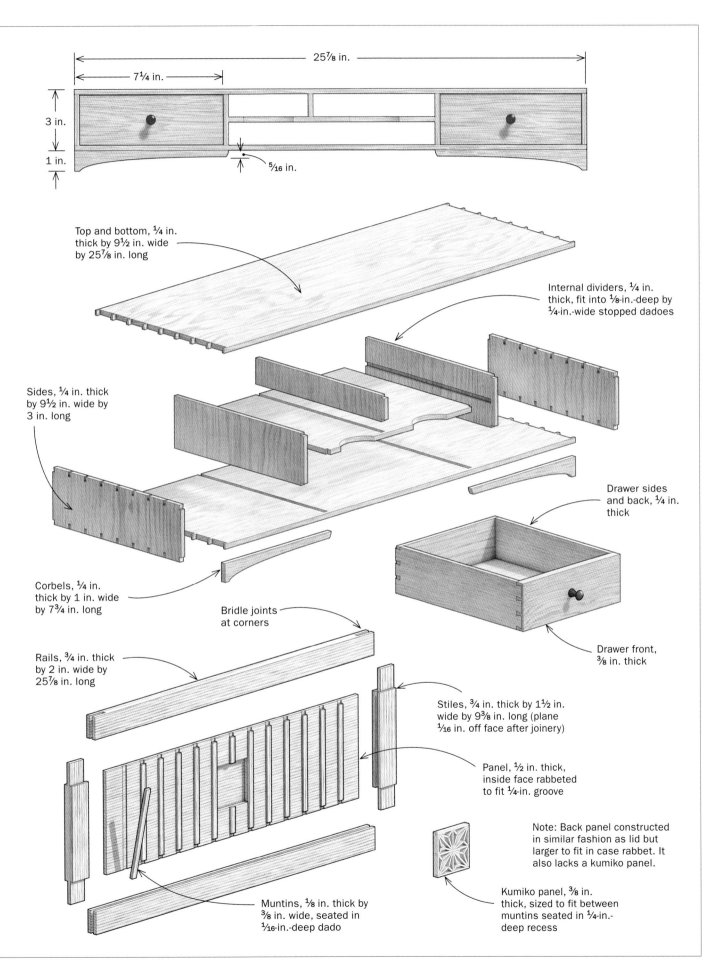

25⁷⁄₈ in.

7¼ in.

3 in.

1 in.

5⁄₁₆ in.

Top and bottom, ¼ in. thick by 9½ in. wide by 25⁷⁄₈ in. long

Internal dividers, ¼ in. thick, fit into ⅛-in.-deep by ¼-in.-wide stopped dadoes

Sides, ¼ in. thick by 9½ in. wide by 3 in. long

Drawer sides and back, ¼ in. thick

Corbels, ¼ in. thick by 1 in. wide by 7¾ in. long

Bridle joints at corners

Drawer front, ⅜ in. thick

Rails, ¾ in. thick by 2 in. wide by 25⁷⁄₈ in. long

Stiles, ¾ in. thick by 1½ in. wide by 9⅜ in. long (plane ¹⁄₁₆ in. off face after joinery)

Panel, ½ in. thick, inside face rabbeted to fit ¼-in. groove

Note: Back panel constructed in similar fashion as lid but larger to fit in case rabbet. It also lacks a kumiko panel.

Muntins, ⅛ in. thick by ⅜ in. wide, seated in ¹⁄₁₆-in.-deep dado

Kumiko panel, ⅜ in. thick, sized to fit between muntins seated in ¼-in.-deep recess

A SIMPLE SOLUTION FOR TAPERED, SPLAYED LEGS

Connecting a round leg to an apron was the biggest challenge in making the base. I ended up putting some simple router jigs to use and cutting the joint while all the parts were still square. To notch the apron for the legs, I made a quick router jig that I could clamp to the apron (**1**). I cut a notch in the jig that matched the notch I wanted in the apron, and then used a flush-trim bit to rout the notch. To create the splay, I just cut a bevel on the ends of the aprons to match and joined the legs to the apron square.

The legs have a notch that I cut using a tenoning jig at the tablesaw. There is also a rabbet around the edges of the slot that allows the leg to join with the apron (**2**). I rout that with a jig similar to the one I used for the aprons.

To turn the legs to their final profile, I made a plug to fit into the slotted end (**3**). This allowed me to mount the legs in the lathe (**4**), and once I had turned the first leg, the plug acted as a template for sizing the remaining legs (**5**).

At first I envisioned unobtrusive hinges but opted instead for hand-forged hardware, which offered a nice surprise waiting inside.

I started with the case, where the challenge was making an inset door that swung down to create a flat writing surface. The key was adding a false bottom to the case interior and coving the actual case bottom to provide clearance for the door. The interior of the desk was outfitted with a hanging gallery for stationery and such. Attaching it to the case top allowed for deeper usable space below it. At first I envisioned unobtrusive hinges but opted instead for hand-forged hardware, which offered a nice surprise waiting inside. Splayed tapered legs are easy to draw, but a little tougher to build. After some thought, I came up with a way to connect the legs to the base with bridle joints while the stock was still square.

The desk now sits in a sunny nook at the top of our stairs. More than just occupying wall space, the desk (along with a chair) transformed an unused space into a sun-filled study. When making furniture, I'd always thought in terms of making things, but the notion of having the ability to transform the spaces we live in and not just decorate them was an eye-opening thought that I've kept in mind ever since.

PLAY IT LOUD

Yes, I know, quiet but not silent. That's a wonderful thing, and if I had to stick with just one theme in my work, and in my life for that matter, that would be it. However, every now and then, I guess it's okay to break out. A while back, as my daughter gained an interest in vinyl records, I picked up a cheap suitcase-style record player so she could give it a spin. Needless to say, the low-quality cartridge and small built-in speaker produced a small, tinny sound at best. Obviously not impressed, she was beginning to wonder what all the fuss was about. So I made it a mission to put a stereo together that would restore her faith in old school hi-fi.

It also offered the opportunity to resurrect the stereo console listening days of my youth, where I'd sit with my ear up to our Zenith® for hours. I wanted a compact piece that would fit nicely in a bedroom or dorm room but still fill up the space with some serious sound. I knew I'd be sacrificing stereo separation by housing both speakers in a single cabinet, but it would still be light-years better than the pair of tiny computer speakers that I call my home stereo today.

Inside the console is a no-frills, good-quality turntable. To make the stereo a little more versatile, I found a small receiver that had Bluetooth input as well as a phono input. That way, both vinyl and an iPhoneSM were equally capable of providing the source of the music. It was also a great excuse to put kumiko to work, this time in the form of a speaker grill. Right now, a pair of bookshelf speakers lives inside the cabinet, but I have my eye on some custom speaker components for my next effort. Altogether the console can fill a room nicely with sound, but even when turned off, the volume is still turned up.

CHAPTER 7

TABLES

Atable is no more than a flat surface of a certain size and shape that is suspended a certain distance from the floor. How you go about getting that surface where it needs to go is where all of the fun starts. Level and sturdy is the goal, but there are a lot of ways to get there. In the three tables I've included here, I've barely begun to scratch the surface of possibilities.

There is another aspect to a table. Compared to most furniture forms, it's the form we come in contact with most frequently. Yes, we sit in a chair, but once we're in it, we don't really notice anything but its comfort, or lack thereof. We sit *at* a table though. It's in front of us. We eat at it, type at it, work at it. We talk at the table, think at it, maybe drink at it, wake up to it, or stay up late at it. We live with it. It's there for holidays and birthdays, homework and science projects.

A kitchen or dinner table doesn't need to be fancy to do its job well, though a little personality is a good thing as long as it's sturdy and well built. Other tables, such as side, coffee, or entry tables, usually serve to add a little more flavor to a room. They can offer a fun opportunity to experiment and to get a little more creative than you might with other furniture forms.

A SEWING TABLE THAT ALMOST WASN'T

My first thought was to make something quick—just legs, aprons, and a top— so I could move on to something "more important."

This table is one of those projects that almost didn't get made. Rachel, my wife, had asked for a small, portable table for her sewing machine. My first thought was to make something quick—just legs, aprons, and a top—so I could move on to something "more important." At this point in my woodworking journey I always seemed to be trying to get a project out of the way in order to get to the good stuff. But this table represents a turning point in my approach to everything I tackle in the shop.

John Tetreault, a good friend and a great woodworker, always seemed to be working on things he was excited about. He even approached the need for a new toilet paper holder with his usual passion and ended up creating a crazy wonderful holder from steam-bent wood and a boulder. It occurred to me that maybe it wasn't the projects he was working on, but his approach to them. For John, every project was that "more important" project that I could never ever seem to get to. So this time around, I stopped and took a minute to think about how John would approach the table. The answer, of course, is that he would invest just as much thought and passion into this project as any other—and end up with a great piece while having a fun time making it.

So I thought about how I could make this table a little more interesting to build and a little more enjoyable to use. A couple of rough sketches and I had an idea in my head. I headed to the shop armed with just that and got to work. I knew the size of the top and the basic height. Because it was intended as a perch for a sewing machine, it had to be lower than a regular worktable. That meant there wasn't room for a drawer or a wide apron. A light arched apron with a floating top sprang to mind and I took it from there. All of the joinery except the mortises was handled at the bandsaw. Draw-bore pins turned an otherwise difficult glue-up into a clamp-free affair. I worked fast, trusting intuition, and didn't worry about any of the voices that are usually muttering in my head while I work.

As I expected, the design suffered a bit from my jumping right into building. The side rail tenons were a little fat, and the arched rail tenons were just low of center. The grain of the parts wasn't exactly as I would have planned had I not been using what I had lying around the shop. But in spite of its shortcomings, there was life to the table, a spark that is so easily stamped out by overthinking a project. On later attempts (I've made several) it was easy enough to address those errors, but that spark of life that is often so difficult to

That original table with its quiet personality brightens our home every day.

capture lived on with each successive build. That original table with its quiet personality brightens our home every day. While Rachel puts it to use most often as a sewing table, it serves very well as a side table, a small writing desk, or even a TV tray.

On the latest version, I fixed the joinery issues that had bothered me, but I didn't really know what to do with the side rails. The fact that it was meant to be a portable table gave me the idea to treat the side rails as handles and wrap them with cord. It was an idea I'd put to use in a clunky, heavy-handed way on the rolling base I'd made for my tool chest. So this was a chance to fix what bothered me about that project as well.

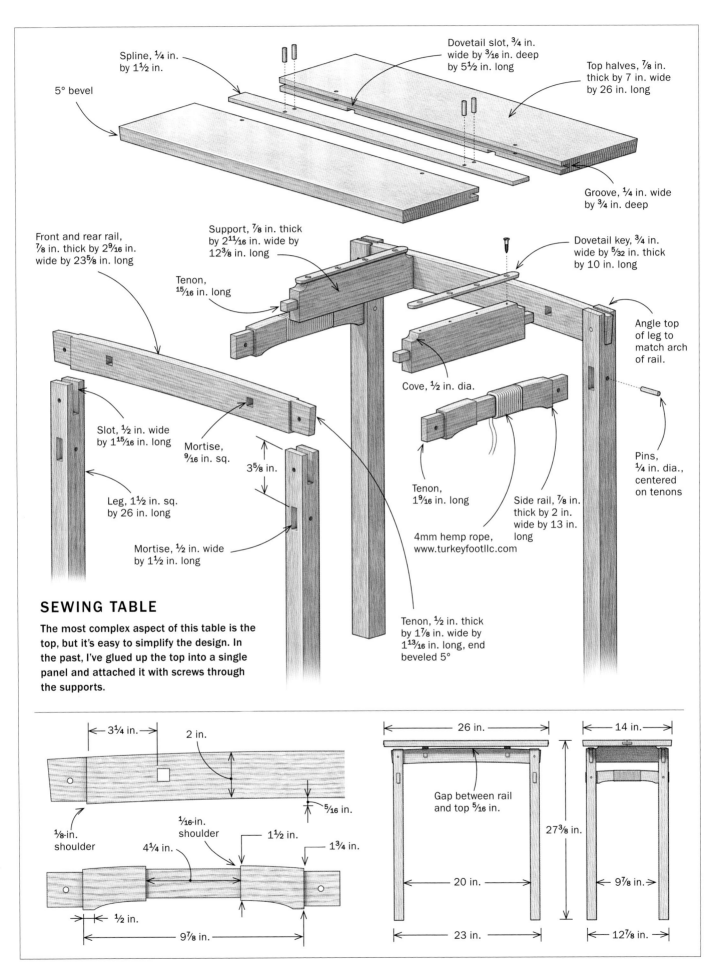

Spline, ¼ in. by 1½ in.

Dovetail slot, ¾ in. wide by ³⁄₁₆ in. deep by 5½ in. long

Top halves, ⅞ in. thick by 7 in. wide by 26 in. long

5° bevel

Groove, ¼ in. wide by ¾ in. deep

Front and rear rail, ⅞ in. thick by 2⁹⁄₁₆ in. wide by 23⅝ in. long

Support, ⅞ in. thick by 2¹¹⁄₁₆ in. wide by 12⅜ in. long

Dovetail key, ¾ in. wide by ⁵⁄₃₂ in. thick by 10 in. long

Tenon, ¹⁵⁄₁₆ in. long

Angle top of leg to match arch of rail.

Slot, ½ in. wide by 1¹⁵⁄₁₆ in. long

Cove, ½ in. dia.

Mortise, ⁹⁄₁₆ in. sq.

3⅝ in.

Leg, 1½ in. sq. by 26 in. long

Tenon, 1⁹⁄₁₆ in. long

Side rail, ⅞ in. thick by 2 in. wide by 13 in. long

Pins, ¼ in. dia., centered on tenons

Mortise, ½ in. wide by 1½ in. long

4mm hemp rope, www.turkeyfootllc.com

SEWING TABLE

The most complex aspect of this table is the top, but it's easy to simplify the design. In the past, I've glued up the top into a single panel and attached it with screws through the supports.

Tenon, ½ in. thick by 1⅞ in. wide by 1¹³⁄₁₆ in. long, end beveled 5°

3¼ in.

2 in.

5⁄₁₆ in.

⅛-in. shoulder

¹⁄₁₆-in. shoulder

1½ in.

4¼ in.

1¾ in.

½ in.

9⅞ in.

26 in.

14 in.

Gap between rail and top ⁵⁄₁₆ in.

27⅜ in.

20 in.

9⅞ in.

23 in.

12⅞ in.

CLAMP-FREE JOINERY

The bridle joint is one you'll find a lot of uses for. You can knock it out fairly easily by hand, but I usually tackle it at the bandsaw. Start by cutting the slots in the legs. It's easier to fit the tenon to the slot rather than the other way around. Set the fence to one face of the slot and make the first cut. Then flip the leg for the second cut to ensure a centered slot (**1**).

For a smooth, accurate cut, make sure your blade is sharp and aligned to the rip fence. Also, it helps to go slow. If it's done correctly, you should end up with a surface that's almost as smooth as one cut from a tablesaw.

Drill out most of the waste using a ½-in.-dia. Forstner bit, which matches the slot width. Then square the slot with a chisel, working in from each face (**2**). Undercutting the joint in the center guarantees that there won't be any material to keep the tenon from fully seating in the slot.

To make the tenons, start with the shoulders and then cut the cheeks (**3**). Use a test piece to sneak up on a snug fit. When making fine adjustments to the bandsaw fence, be sure to cut off the end of the test piece to prevent the blade from wandering into the previous cut and giving you a false reading. When sawing by hand, use a shoulder plane to dial in the final fit.

The bridle joint is a difficult joint to clamp because it must be pulled together in two directions. The protruding ends of the parts only complicate the situation. So I turn to drawbore pins, which pull the joint together as they are driven in. I used the technique for the side-rail mortise and tenons on the table as well. The trick is to drill slightly offset holes through the parts.

Start by drilling a hole through the mortises and then dry-fit the parts and use a drill bit to mark for the hole in the tenons (**4**). For the mortise and tenons, offset the mark roughly 1/32 in. toward the shoulder of the tenon. For the bridle joint, which needs to be clamped both across the joint and down, offset the hole at a 45° angle (**5**). This way, the joint is pulled in both directions as the pin is driven in. I use a dowel plate to make the pins (**6**), starting with straight-grained stock to keep the pins from breaking under the stress of pulling the joint together (**7**).

4 **5**

6

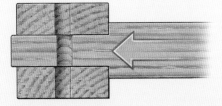

Driving a pin through the offset holes in the mortise and tenon pulls the joint tightly together.

7

Acknowledge the successes, but don't forget the frustrations—they both lead you down a path to better work.

The final aspect of the table that I wanted to address was how the top was fastened to the base. On the original, I simply drove screws up though the table supports into the top. The holes were visible only on the bottom of the rails, which wasn't really a problem, but it was inelegant enough to prompt a better solution. I had recently made a cutting board that consisted of two halves joined together with dovetailed cleats. I figured I could put that idea to use here as well.

So to sum up the influences so far: a nice spark of a table, frustration at grain and joinery miscues in the past, a cool handle idea that had been executed in poor fashion, and a cutting board. It's a good illustration that the notion of evolving design isn't as elegant and linear as you might think it to be. Just keep all of those angels and demons tucked away in your head and let them show you the way forward. Acknowledge the successes, but don't forget the frustrations—they both lead you down a path to better work. Good design is not genius; it's part fun and play and part toughing it out and maintaining a critical eye while forgiving faults. And it's fun. Yes, I mentioned that twice.

Building the table is straightforward, though the joinery is a little unusual (see pp. 186–187). There are some bridle joints and through-tenons, all of which are left proud of the surface. Drawbore pins pull everything together for a clamp-free glue-up. If you'd like, you can leave out the glue altogether. Arched rails and a beveled tabletop add lift, but the table remains a stout little thing.

THAT'S A WRAP

Hemp cord adds a nice texture to the table and encourages interaction. I cut a shallow notch in the rail to recess the cord just a little bit. I also pre-finish the rails first. Start by making a few wraps over the end of the cord to secure it in place (**1**). Make sure the end is on the inside face of the rail, and trim it after four or five wraps.

As you near the end, insert a loop of wire under the cord for the last few wraps (**2**). Trim the end of the cord, leaving an extra 2 in., and feed it through the wire loop. Use a pair of pliers to pull the loop under the wraps to secure the end (**3**). Trim the end off between the wraps with a sharp knife (**4**).

It was the first time I had been prompted to push beyond my comfort zone and explore the style untethered to any specific design.

A MISSING LINK

I received the following note from a client (my brother actually): "I want a table in the Arts and Crafts style, but something I've never seen before." It was an interesting request. Stevie, my little brother, is as passionate about Arts and Crafts furniture and pottery as I am, and he had just tracked down a crate of vintage Rookwood tiles that had been sitting in a basement in Cincinnati for who knows how long. He was looking to put them to use in a few tabletops. He requested a pair of smaller tables fashioned after a tile-top Stickley side table (below), but he wanted something different for a larger entry table.

I don't recall whether he requested the drawers or if they were just something that

I wanted to include. Either way, I had arrived at the idea of a box of drawers on a base. Feeling that I had stumbled onto a fairly original idea for a table, I was a little disappointed to find later that it closely resembled a hall table by Greene & Greene that resided in the Gamble House in Pasadena—a house that I had toured on numerous occasions and the subject of more than a few books that I own. Clearly a case of embedded memory rather than blinding genius.

Regardless of the inspiration, it was the first time I had been prompted to push beyond my comfort zone and explore the style untethered to any specific design. While still firmly rooted in the Arts and Crafts style, it definitely points the way forward to much of the work that has followed it. While I don't consider my current work to fit cleanly into any established style, the Arts and Crafts aesthetic is built into the bones of much of it.

A REFUGE IN THE STORM

I'm passionate about tables but must admit that I'm not fond of the term *dining table*. A dining table was the table in the fancy room of the house that I grew up in. The one we could never eat at unless company was over. The one relegated to card games and jigsaw puzzles and homework on occasion. To me, *dinner table* is a more apt description. In a lot of ways the dinner table is at the heart of our home now. It's where we eat together, though less and less frequently these days, unfortunately. It's where we celebrate birthdays and forge through the traumas that everyday life can throw at us. In that way, our dinner table is the foundation of our home and of our family. I think it's true for a lot of other families as well, and because of that, the table we choose to build has the potential to contribute to the end user in a lot of different ways.

I tend to be fairly agnostic about most aspects of woodworking, whether it's the tools you use, the methods in which you work, the style you choose to build in, or the space that you call a shop. But here's where I draw the line, because there are some important things to get right, things that can make a big difference in your life. More than anything else, making a dinner or kitchen table is the place and time to forget about fancy —to forget about impressing neighbors, or the boss, or the extended family you see once a year that always seems to have an opinion about the way you are raising your children or how much you should be getting paid. I know. Impressing all of those people with the results of your efforts, to explain and validate all of those hours you spend in the shop doing who knows what, is a tempting thing.

This table is not for them. It is for you. For your family, whether that means just you and a roommate in a small apartment, or a growing family in an overstuffed, undersized house. Amidst all of that change and uncertainty, here is an anchor, a refuge amidst the storms of life that can rage around you. Yes, you can make do with a folding table, or a box on the floor in front of the TV. But make a table. Don't start with a design or a particular style, but with a feeling, a thought of what that foundation needs to offer you. My particular answer to that question may not be—and probably won't be— yours. But start there and don't stop until you find an idea that answers the question. Then let that idea begin

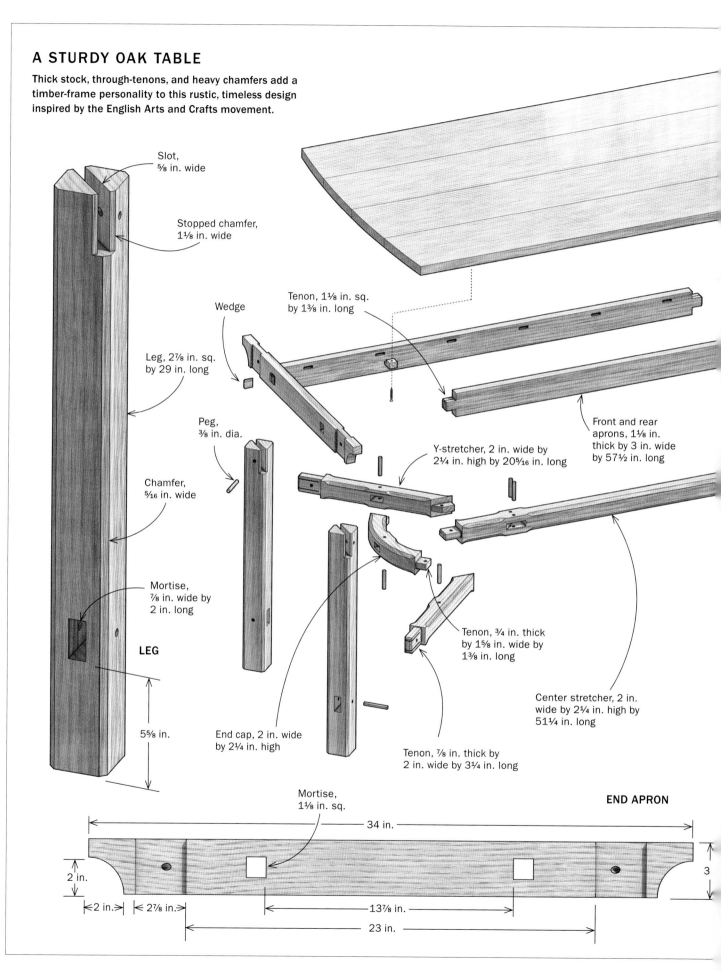

A STURDY OAK TABLE

Thick stock, through-tenons, and heavy chamfers add a timber-frame personality to this rustic, timeless design inspired by the English Arts and Crafts movement.

Slot,
⅝ in. wide

Stopped chamfer,
1⅛ in. wide

Wedge

Tenon, 1⅛ in. sq.
by 1⅜ in. long

Leg, 2⅞ in. sq.
by 29 in. long

Peg,
⅜ in. dia.

Chamfer,
5⁄16 in. wide

Y-stretcher, 2 in. wide by
2¼ in. high by 20 5⁄16 in. long

Front and rear
aprons, 1⅛ in.
thick by 3 in. wide
by 57½ in. long

Mortise,
⅞ in. wide by
2 in. long

LEG

Tenon, ¾ in. thick
by 1⅝ in. wide by
1⅜ in. long

Center stretcher, 2 in.
wide by 2¼ in. high by
51¼ in. long

5⅝ in.

End cap, 2 in. wide
by 2¼ in. high

Tenon, ⅞ in. thick by
2 in. wide by 3¼ in. long

Mortise,
1⅛ in. sq.

END APRON

34 in.

2 in.

3

2 in.

2⅞ in.

13⅞ in.

23 in.

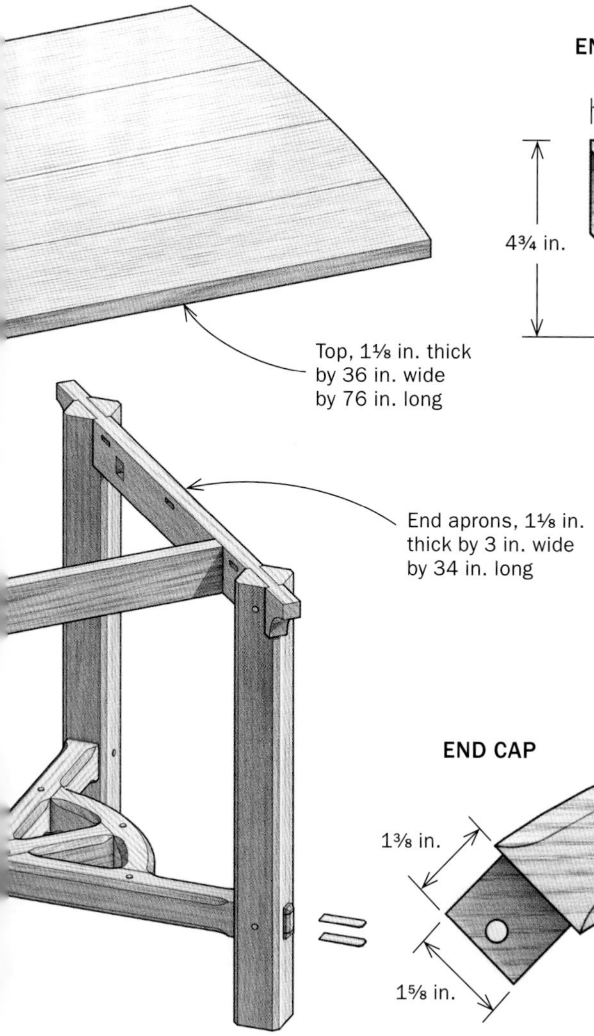
Top, 1⅛ in. thick
by 36 in. wide
by 76 in. long
End aprons, 1⅛ in.
thick by 3 in. wide
by 34 in. long

END-CAP BLANK

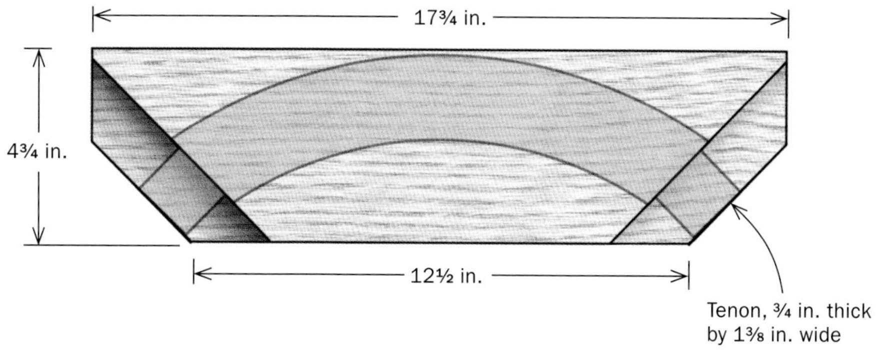
17¾ in.
4¾ in.
12½ in.
Tenon, ¾ in. thick
by 1⅜ in. wide

END CAP

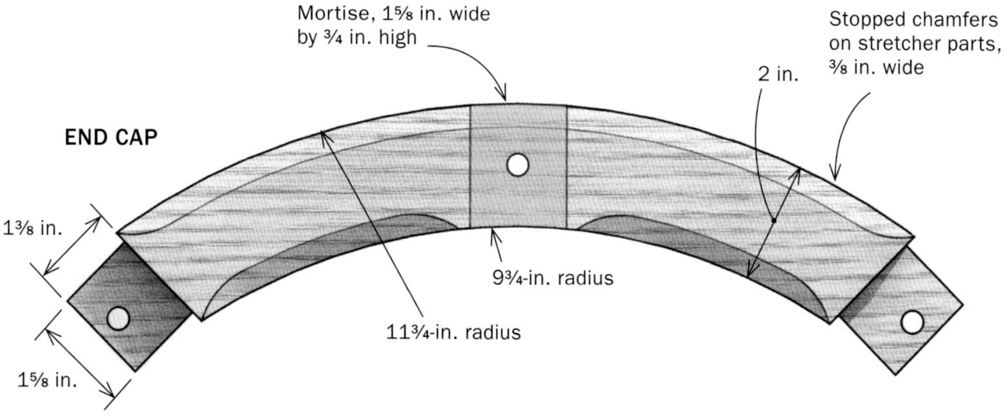
Mortise, 1⅝ in. wide
by ¾ in. high
Stopped chamfers
on stretcher parts,
⅜ in. wide
2 in.
1⅜ in.
9¾-in. radius
11¾-in. radius
1⅝ in.

CENTER STRETCHER

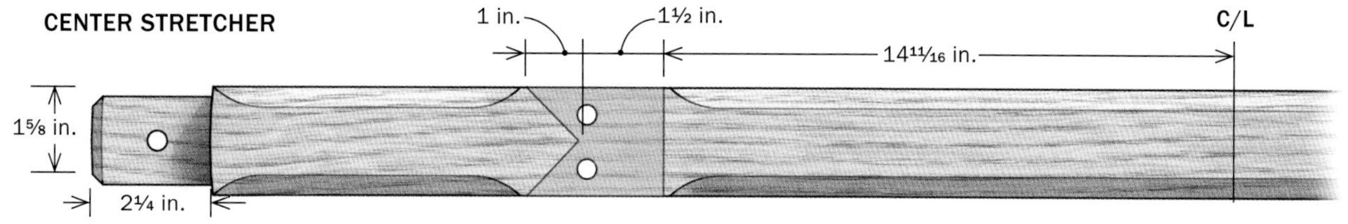
1 in.
1½ in.
C/L
14¹¹⁄₁₆ in.
1⅝ in.
2¼ in.

Y-STRETCHER

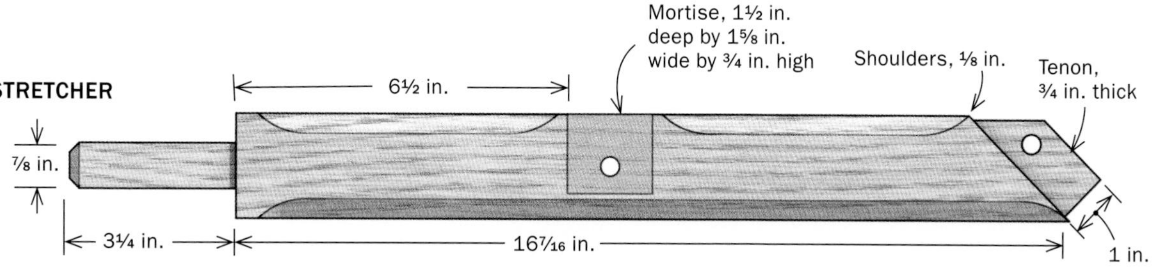
Mortise, 1½ in.
deep by 1⅝ in.
wide by ¾ in. high
6½ in.
Shoulders, ⅛ in.
Tenon,
¾ in. thick
⅞ in.
3¼ in.
16⁷⁄₁₆ in.
1 in.

to grow into a vision that leads to a design. And if you're building for someone else, this is the time to listen, to get past the circled pictures in the Pottery Barn® catalog, and to get to the heart of what they're really after.

We had a Shaker-style trestle table that served us well for many years, but although it did a good job of supporting items 30 in. off the floor, it didn't contribute a lot more to the conversation. The top was too thin, and it had a folding leaf that I had permanently secured in the up position. It was also the only oddball in a room otherwise dominated by Arts and Crafts. Not that the style was overly important, but I had slowly begun to establish a sense of place in the room with each piece that I had made, and the dinner table was the only holdout from a previous time.

So a lot of what I envisioned for a new dinner table was similar to the furniture that was already filling the room. A sense of mass and permanence, a sense of history. Maybe not history exactly, but a resonance of the past, a warm comfort and familiarity. An affinity for weathering abuse. The strength of a stone foundation or a timber-frame barn. More specifically, the idea began to manifest itself in certain features. A thick top, stout legs, the tenacity of white oak, heavy chamfers.

That trail led to the idea of a hayrake table, a product of the English Arts and Crafts movement that predated and heavily influenced the American movement. My table is

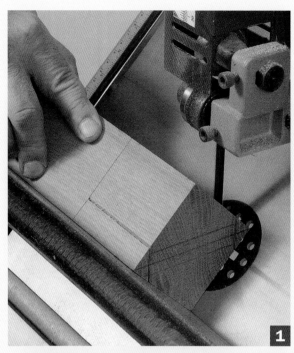

BRIDLE JOINT ON THE BIAS

The first step is to create a flat on either side of the slot. You can cut the flats with a handsaw or tilt your bandsaw to 45° and make quick work of it (**1**). Then cut the bottom with a backsaw (**2**). To make the slot, head back to the bandsaw, cut one cheek, and then rotate the stock to cut the second cheek (**3**). Drill out the waste with a Forstner bit and chop the base line square (**4**). From here, treat it just as you would a normal bridle joint.

THE HAYRAKE STRETCHER

The end cap is the highlight of the lower stretcher. To get to it, the first step is to connect the angled arms (or Y-stretchers) to the center stretcher. Cut a 45° miter on one end of each arm, and then use a miter gauge and dado blade to cut the tenon cheeks (**1**). Next cut the shoulder on the inside of the tenon at the bandsaw (**2**).

Mortise the center stretcher and angle the outside end of the mortise using a guide block clamped to the stretcher (**3**). While you're at it, mortise a short cutoff in the same way to use as a setup block for sizing the cap.

The end cap starts as a wide blank. Miter the ends and cut the tenon cheeks in the same way as the arms. Insert the arms into the setup block to transfer the mortise locations onto the end-cap blank (**4**). Cut the tenon ends and fit the end-cap blank into the arm assembly. Use a beam compass or trammel points to mark the curve of the end cap (**5**). After mortising the end cap for the tenon on the end of the center stretcher, cut out the curve (**6**).

Assemble the arms to the center stretcher and set the end cap on the assembly to locate the curved tenon shoulders (**7**). Cut the tenon, starting with a square shoulder, and then use a chisel to pare to the curved knife line. Sneak up on the fit until the joint fully seats (**8**). Don't sweat it if the fit isn't perfect—this style forgives a gap here and there.

4

5

6

7

8

based loosely on a library table by Sidney Barnsley, one of the pioneers of English Arts and Crafts design. Its solid base resembles a timber-frame structure more than a piece of furniture. The parts are oversize, with solid square legs, a heavily chamfered stretcher, and a thick top. The joinery is larger in scale as well, with proud tenons and pins. Draw-bore pegs pull everything together and add to its girded look. I wouldn't call it rustic or primitive in style, though those descriptions aren't that far off. Solid and basic maybe, but with an architectural order to it as well, which is highlighted by the lower stretcher, its curved ends resembling a traditional hayrake and giving the table its name.

Another distinctive feature of the table, though it may not be apparent at first, is the orientation of the legs. They are at 45° instead of parallel to the edges of the tabletop. This adds an extra step to cutting the bridle joint at the top of the legs but simplifies hayrake stretcher joinery, which is well worth the trade-off.

PULL IT ALL TOGETHER

Draw-bore pins do away with what would be a nightmare clamping situation. Drill through the mortise and transfer the center of the hole onto the tenon with a brad-point bit (**1**). Then drill a hole through the tenon, offsetting it $\frac{1}{32}$ in. toward the shoulder. This offset will pull the joint together tightly as the peg is driven in (**2**). Rout a chamfer along the parts, stopping short of the intersections, and fare that portion with a chisel. Fasten the top to the base with wooden buttons (**3**).

CHAPTER 8

FINISHING

Finishing can be stressful at the end of a big build when the last thing you want to do is mess things up. It seems to be every woodworker's least favorite task but most popular topic of study. It's a very broad subject, but you don't have to know everything about finishing to be successful.

Here, I'll cover the two basic finishes I use; between them, they handle almost all of the finishing challenges you'll face. The first finish is shellac. This finish can be intimidating, but once you get to know it, it will make life easier for you. I use shellac on its own for small projects and in conjunction with varnish in a couple of different ways. The second finish is a wiping varnish, which is my go-to finish for larger projects. It's a versatile finish that can offer the look of an oil and wax finish or can be built up for a higher shine and maximum protection.

We tend to equate the final finish with the final look of the project, but there's a lot more that goes into a successful project than just the finish—everything from lumber selection to preparing surfaces, with the actual finishing step playing a fairly minor role. Because we have control over the process at every step, if we do each task well, the finishing portion of the project should be quick and painless.

FINISHING BEGINS AT THE LUMBERYARD

The finishes I use are designed to highlight the grain and luster of the wood. Unfortunately, they also do a good job of highlighting machine marks, sanding scratches, and tearout.

The finishes I use are simple. I can get away with that because I have control over lumber selection and grain placement. The ideal is to get all of your parts from the same tree, which means you'll have perfect grain and color match locked in at the very beginning. Short of that, you can still build a sense of order into a piece by getting similar parts from the same board. In this way, there's no need to delve into dyes and stains to make up for mismatched boards.

Another important concern is how you're using the parts of a board in a piece. Understanding plainsawn, riftsawn, and quartersawn stock and how they can affect the look of a piece affords you an important tool in directing the final outcome. Using straight grain for legs, dividers, and doorframes can add order to a piece and highlight its structure. Wild, swirling grain can pop door panels. Drawer fronts can go either way, depending on the effect you're after. Spend some time and thought at this stage and you've already locked down the foundation for a great finish. Skip it, and you've built in a lot of problems and most likely compromised the rest of the work to follow. I know that may sound harsh, but once you begin to see what good lumber selection can do, you won't turn back.

The next key to a good finish is surface prep. The finishes I use are designed to highlight the grain and luster of the wood. Unfortunately, they also do a good job of highlighting machine marks, sanding scratches, and tearout. Don't put off surface prep until the project is assembled—a lot of parts can be more easily surfaced ahead of time. Do a good job of it and you'll thank yourself later.

I don't wait to start finishing either. The more prefinishing I can do during building, the less I have to do later and the easier time I'll have of it. Any part that won't get planed or sanded flush after glue-up is a candidate for prefinishing. Also, areas that would be difficult to finish once assembled, like door panels and the insides of cases and boxes, are best handled ahead of time. On parts with proud joinery like dovetails or through-tenons, presealing the end grain ensures that any excess glue won't cause blotching once the final finish is applied later.

So choose lumber carefully, use grain thoughtfully, prep perfectly, and get a head start by prefinishing. After that, the actual "finishing" portion of the job is mostly done and your project is definitely on its way to a finish you'll be happy with.

START WITH GOOD WOOD AND USE IT WELL

Not every lumberyard is going to have flitches of lumber from the same log, though it's great when you can get it. The nearest source of flitch-sawn lumber for me, Irion Lumber (facing page), is about four hours away. It's worth the trip on a big project, but short of that, I'll keep an eye out for matched boards within a stack at my local lumberyard. Another option (which is becoming more common) is to track down portable saw-mill operators in your area. You'll have to wait a while for the wood to dry, but you can often get matched lumber for a fraction of the price.

The way you use your lumber can have a big effect on the finished piece. Rather than mark out a board for maximum yield, I'll take the time to figure out the best areas for each piece. For the small table shown here, I wanted quiet, straight rift-sawn grain for the legs (**1**), continuous grain around the aprons and drawer (**2**), and a book-matched top with tight grain at the edges for a seamless glue-up (**3**). I was able to get all of the parts from the same board by being strategic about which section of the board each of the parts was coming from (**4**).

A BEAUTIFUL FAST FINISH

Shellac is one of those finishes that a lot of woodworkers tend to shy away from. If you've ever tried to brush it on straight from the can, you can probably understand why. And if you've read about the fine art of French polishing, you'd be forgiven if you were left feeling a little intimidated. The truth is that shellac is a great fast-drying finish that's easy to apply and perfect for small projects and last-minute gifts that need to get out the door quickly. I have a simple technique that yields a nice satin finish that's friendly to the touch in about 30 minutes.

One of the funky things about using shellac is that it's not ready to use straight out of the can. Not only that, often shellac doesn't even come in a can. You can buy it in flake form and mix it yourself. Either way, getting the right consistency is not difficult. For premixed shellac in a can, I prefer SealCoat® from Zinsser®. It's a light-colored shellac with the naturally occurring wax removed, which makes the finish more durable and allows other finishes to adhere to it. To use it, simply dilute it 1:1 with denatured alcohol.

Mixing your own shellac from flakes is a little more involved, but it has its advantages. Shellac in flake form has a longer shelf life and is available in a variety of colors. In addition, I've found that it dries faster than premixed, which speeds the finishing process.

The key to success with shellac is building up just a thin layer of finish. However, that means that any mill marks, tearout, or sanding scratches will show up in the final finish, so getting flat and smooth is a must. For open-pore woods like oak, sand to 400-grit; for closed-pore woods such as cherry and maple, sand to 600-grit or beyond.

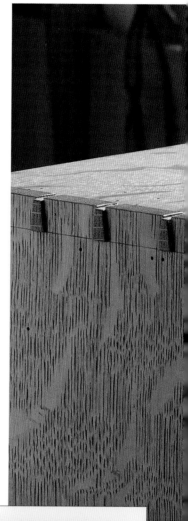

SHELLAC FROM FLAKES

The challenge when mixing your own shellac is to get the right ratio of shellac to alcohol. The easiest way I've found is to do it without weighing or measuring. Just add some flakes to a jar and fill it with denatured alcohol to the top of the flakes (1).

Let the mix stand overnight or until the flakes are fully dissolved. You'll be left with a very heavy solution of shellac. To make a workable solution, use a baster to add one part shellac to four parts alcohol in a fresh jar (2).

SHELLAC, STEP BY STEP

For best results, thin the finish by half with alcohol (**1**). Start the finishing process by wiping on a thin coat over the entire surface using a clean cotton rag (**2**). The finish should soak in and dry quickly. Store the rag in a closed container to keep it from drying out and you can use it indefinitely.

No matter how smooth the surface was after sanding, it will probably feel rough after the first coat. This is not a bad thing. The initial coat of finish performed the important task of saturating the wood fibers. A quick sand with the grit you left off with should result in the same smooth surface (**3**). The big difference is that the fibers are now locked in place and the surface should stay fairly smooth throughout the rest of the finishing process.

The key to avoiding drips and runs is to wipe on the finish in thin coats (**4**). Shellac is a solvent-based finish, which means that wiping on a coat will partially dissolve the coats you've already applied. Because of this, it's important not to wipe back and forth over wet surfaces or you'll run the risk of lifting off the finish as you're trying to build it up. Instead, wipe the finish in straight, slightly overlapping coats, and wait for the surface to dry before applying additional coats. This might sound like a time-consuming process, but the finish dries so fast that by the time you finish coating all the surfaces of a project, chances are the first surfaces are dry enough to continue finishing. However, after three or four coats, the finish will begin to stay sticky

longer and dry more slowly. At this point, wait for 10 minutes or so and let the finish cure.

Before continuing, check to see if there are any rough areas from raised grain or dust, and scuff-sand with fine sandpaper as necessary (5). After another coat or two you should be close to having enough finish on the project. Even though I'm aiming for a satin finish, I apply enough shellac so that it's slightly glossier than I'd like. This is a good indication that there's enough finish to offer a moderate amount of protection and durability in the long run. The finish at this point might be a little streaky or have a

slightly uneven shine, but that's okay. The next step of the process will even everything out.

The final step is to rub out the finish. I do this by applying paste wax with fine steel wool (6). The steel wool should remove any minor roughness, but you can hit any problem areas with 600-grit sandpaper and continue. To make the wax easier to apply, dip the steel wool in mineral spirits first. This will dilute the wax and let it spread more smoothly. Finally, buff the surface with a clean rag to reveal a beautiful satin finish (7).

WIPING VARNISH FOR LARGER PROJECTS

While you can brush on a varnish for a gloppy, glossy finish, that's not exactly the look I'm going for on my furniture.

Although fast drying is good on small projects, the slower drying time of wiping varnish is actually a plus on bigger projects. It allows you to cover a larger area before the finish begins to dry. Also, an oil-based varnish offers more protection than a shellac finish.

While you can brush on a varnish for a gloppy, glossy finish, that's not exactly the look I'm going for on my furniture. For me, the ideal finish for handmade furniture is a low-luster finish that lets the beauty of the wood shine through. The easiest way to get there is to wipe on thin coats and slowly build to the sheen you want. A wiping varnish, as the name implies, allows you to do just that.

A brand I typically use is Waterlox®, a tung-oil-based varnish that builds quickly, levels well, and adds a beautiful amber tone to the work. For lighter woods where the amber color may be too much, I turn to Minwax® Wipe-On Poly. It builds a little more slowly but is the lightest in color of the varnishes that I've tried. With either product, or other brands for that matter, the application method is the same.

SEAL, SMOOTH, AND BUILD

The job of the first coat of wiping varnish is to seal the wood, not to build up a finish just yet. Slop it on with a rag or brush. Don't worry about making a mess, but make sure you saturate the wood (**1**). After 10 minutes or so, wipe the entire surface dry and wait 24 hours before moving on.

The next step is to level the surface. The easiest way to do this is to apply a thin coat of finish (**2**) and wet-sand with P400-grit paper (**3**). Wipe the surface dry afterward and let it dry overnight. The result is a sealed, smooth starting point from which to begin applying the remaining coats.

Build the finish in a series of thin coats. Start with a circular motion to apply the varnish. Then level the finish with light strokes in the direction of the grain to even out the finish without completely wiping it off (**4**). Four to six of these light coats should build up enough finish to protect the wood without encasing it in a heavy film. The thin coats should dry quickly enough to allow a couple of coats a day.

On smaller projects I apply wax with steel wool, rubbing out and waxing the piece in one step. On larger surfaces, though, it can be hard to see the scratch pattern created by the steel wool, and it's easy to end up with an uneven sheen.

In those cases, I'll rub out the surface before applying the wax by adding mineral spirits to the steel wool (**5**). When wiping on the wax, I dampen the cloth with mineral spirits first as well. It thins the wax and allows me to apply an even coat that's easier to buff when dry (**6**).

COMBINING FINISHES

On pieces with a shellac finish, adding an extra layer of varnish on wear areas like shelves and tabletops will increase protection from moisture. Wipe on thin coats and rub out the finish as you normally would (**1**).

On varnished pieces, you can start off with a wash coat of shellac to seal the surface and to prevent glue from sticking and causing blotching. Wipe on a thin coat and sand it once it dries (**2**). The surface won't look a lot different than an unfinished surface, but the varnish will build much more quickly than when applied to bare wood.

SHELLAC AND VARNISH MAKE A GOOD TEAM

One of the special characteristics of shellac is that it can stick to most finishes and most finishes can stick to it.

Shellac and varnish are great finishes on their own, but you can take advantage of their individual benefits by using them together as well. What makes this possible is that varnish adheres to shellac. For that reason, you can lay down a quick washcoat of shellac under a varnished project, or top off a shellac project with varnish in just the areas where you want more protection.

While shellac is great on small projects, there are times when I need a little more protection in certain areas than shellac alone can offer. A small side table is a perfect place to use shellac, but I'll follow that with a few coats of varnish on just the top, where the extra protection is needed. For a tea chest that sits on a live-edge base, I'll add wiping varnish to just the base, where it's likely to come in contact with teapots and cups as well as moisture.

Another way I use shellac is as a washcoat under a piece to be varnished. I work a lot with proud joinery and one of the challenges is to keep glue off of the outside of the joints. This is especially important on end grain, where the glue can soak in and cause splotching once an oil finish is applied. A quick coat of shellac will seal the surfaces to prevent blotching. It also makes any squeeze-out easier to remove once it's dry. Typically, all I have to do is pop it off with a sharp chisel. The other benefit to starting with shellac is that the varnish will build more quickly. The only downside of using shellac under varnish is that it can slightly reduce the luster on highly figured woods like tiger maple or curly cherry. In those cases, I'll skip the shellac and go straight to varnish.

METRIC EQUIVALENTS

INCHES	CENTIMETERS	MILLIMETERS	INCHES	CENTIMETERS	MILLIMETERS
⅛	0.3	3	13	33.0	330
¼	0.6	6	14	35.6	356
⅜	1.0	10	15	38.1	381
½	1.3	13	16	40.6	406
⅝	1.6	16	17	43.2	432
¾	1.9	19	18	45.7	457
⅞	2.2	22	19	48.3	483
1	2.5	25	20	50.8	508
1¼	3.2	32	21	53.3	533
1½	3.8	38	22	55.9	559
1¾	4.4	44	23	58.4	584
2	5.1	51	24	61	610
2½	6.4	64	25	63.5	635
3	7.6	76	26	66.0	660
3½	8.9	89	27	68.6	686
4	10.2	102	28	71.7	717
4½	11.4	114	29	73.7	737
5	12.7	127	30	76.2	762
6	15.2	152	31	78.7	787
7	17.8	178	32	81.3	813
8	20.3	203	33	83.8	838
9	22.9	229	34	86.4	864
10	25.4	254	35	88.9	889
11	27.9	279	36	91.4	914
12	30.5	305			

INDEX

If you like this book, you'll love *Fine Woodworking*.

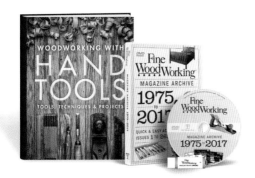